ISIS DUSK

SPECIAL FORCES OPERATIONS IN SYRIA & IRAQ

STEVE STONE

COPYRIGHT

Copyright © by Steve Stone 2016

Steve Stone has asserted his rights under the Copyright, Design and Patents Act, 1988, to be identified as the author of this work.

Published by Digital Dreams Publishing 2016

Author's Note

ISIS Dusk follows on from my first book ISIS Dawn. This second book takes a look at the final phase of the war against ISIS in Iraq & Syria. This time I have focused more on individual operations as opposed to the background to ISIS and the war in Iraq in Syria. Coalition soldiers have died in the process of the war on ISIS. Thankfully, that number has been small but does not take away the tragedy of loss of life and families losing a husband and a father. ISIS will soon be pushed out of Iraq and defeated in Syria, but that does not mean the war on them is finished. They are already moving into Libya and have numerous terror cells lined up around the world to kill as many innocent citizens or 'infidels' as ISIS believes they are. In the hope it is one step closer to creating their own caliphate.

Steve Stone July 2016

ONE – FOREWARD

Iraq February 2016

By the beginning of 2016, there were nearly 250 British soldiers in Iraq a mixture of SAS and SBS personnel. As well as the SAS and SBS, there was also members of the Parachute Regiment and the Special Reconnaissance Regiment. Britain has more than 200 special force soldiers in Iraq under Operation Shader.

Some say we should have seen it coming. After the main forces left following the second Iraq war, Iraq was far from stable. With various factions fighting each other. Removing Saddam Hussein had left a power vacuum and a weak government. Islamic State also known as ISIS saw their opportunity to land grab and of course seize the precious oil wells which would act as a funding stream for them. Under Operation Inherent Resolve commanded by Lt. General Sean MacFarland. British and American air and ground force along with Russian air power have been back in a limited number to try to support Iraqi security forces to get rid of this new and quite worrying threat.

In February 2016 a British, German and U.S. special forces mission was to hunt out terrorist positions outside ISIS-held Mosul and spot weak areas in the network's defences. Mosul is Iraq's second city and was captured by Islamic State in 2014. It is currently home to more than 30,000 fighters who have made good use of the seizure of Iraqi military hardware.

The SAS have been operating in small teams in northern Iraq with other forces to collate intelligence. Operating out of a heavily fortified inner base camp, within a Peshmerga camp, just south west of Mosul, alongside the Euphrates River.

A specials forces team of 25 had mounted up on white old Toyota Hilux's the SAS and SBS troopers wore local scarves and hid assault weapons in the floor of the trucks so as not to alert IS spotters. The small force was about 10 miles south of Mosul when the team found themselves being ambushed with a .50 cal machine gun mounted on an American Humvee and RPGs (Rocket Propelled Grenades). As 30 IS fighters fired on the 25-strong allied Special Forces patrol.

  The SAS and SBS troopers had no choice but to dive out of their almost unprotected trucks and seek cover before firing back with their assault rifles. To buy some time, an eight-man German commando team then obliterated one ISIS position with armour-piercing missiles, killing several enemy gunmen. The outcome was that all thirty IS fighters lay dead after an airstrike was called in killing any survivors.

  During the ferocious firefight three SAS and SBS troops were hurt from fragmentation injuries after an Islamic State RPG detonated nearby. The three soldiers had made a lucky escape with some nasty but not life threatening injuries.

  About 120 SAS operatives in an even more clandestine war has seen the SAS dressing up as ISIS fighters carrying the ISIS flag or ISIS banners. They operate as small units called 'smash' units and travel in civilian pickups. Launching UAVs to gather intelligence and target data. The SAS teams reveal their coordinates to RAF and coalition air forces and are assigned a 'kill box.' The kill box is an area which will not be attacked from the air whilst the SAS are operating within it. The technique of posing as the enemy is an old one, and has been used in WWI and WW II, in Rhodesia, El Salvador and other wars.

  The SAS teams are under U.S. command and operate with U.S.-provided equipment, including unmanned aerial vehicle (UAV) intelligence systems. To undertake this ISIS is partly in on the deception. The hunting down and tracking of terrorists does rely on shifting alliances.

  ISIS still has a command structure and world wide support, locally in parts it is a bit more of a mish mash and some IS fighters want to leave as it is not what they thought it would be.

  This is not too dissimilar to many of the operations special forces from around the world have been involved in. In more conventional raids one Delta and one SEAL operator have paid the ultimate price. ISIS has proven to be a formidable foe and the Iraqi Army initially struggled to hold them back, never mind push them out of occupied areas. The vast amount of training the Iraqi Army has been given from coalition soldiers has helped them to become much more adept at being able to take on ISIS and begin the final campaign to remove them from Mosul and finally out of Iraq. Although, small pockets or terror cells of IS fighters will remain. These will continue to carry out terrorist attacks for some years to come. Libya seems to becoming a new safe haven for ISIS as they have not given up of creating their own caliphate and imposing their inhuman way of life on everyone.

TWO – JOINT OP

Syria May 2015

Delta was down to take part joint operation with us in Eastern Syria. It must be said even as the 'underdogs' in some circles Delta are bloody good at what they do. The operation Delta had been tasked for was to take out Abu Sayyaf a top Islamic State financier. Sayyaf was a Tunisian who the government wanted to question about the terror group's financing. It was Sayyaf who set up a system where private buyers would line up with trucks at oil fields, pay in cash for crude oil, and transport it in their own trucks. The truckers would sell this crude oil at a profit to local, makeshift refineries. This fuel once refined was sold onto either roadside pumping stations or smugglers who would sell it onto more populated areas.

Sayyaf also wanted so that he could be questioned about hostages murdered by Islamic State including Kayla Mueller currently the last known American captive. Sayyaf was given custody of the American aid worker Kayla Mueller in September 2014 after she had suffered by being Islamic State leader Abu Bakr al-Baghdadi's sex slave.

It was also hoped if captured he could be brought to justice and face terrorism charges. JSOC had been tracking Sayyaf since early 2014 due to his importance to Islamic State. The mission had originally been due to be undertaken in March 2015, but poor weather and intelligence issues had delayed it.

We had been sent out to perform reconnaissance on our target several days before. To ensure our participation was kept secret due to ensure no political ramifications. We wore American uniforms and even carried American weapons to keep their participation secret. The American uniforms were not as good as our British ones. We were even flow in by a U.S. V-22 Osprey tilt rotor aircraft. These ungainly looking aircraft with their oversized twin rotors and tilt wing design have become excellent workhorse now its reliability issues have been overcome.

In cities like Raqqa, Syria, where Islamic State is has established its headquarters, people are killed, tortured, detained, and oppressed to ensure they follow Islamic State Doctrine. These victims are not foreigners, but fellow Muslims whom the group has labelled apostates for not adhering to Islamic Sates religious laws. If a man is found drinking or a woman is not correctly veiled they are he beaten. The city has many of its building painted black and Islamic State flags hang all over the city. Earning it the dubious name of "Black Province."

Heavily armed checkpoints control passage into and out of the city. At theses checkpoints people are interrogated and inspected. Anyone who is thought to be a traitor which includes members of rival groups such as Nusrah Front or the Free Syrian Army (FSA). They are arrested and taken away. The streets are patrolled by IS fighters to ensure their laws are met this includes entering homes and schools to check women are correctly veiled. Anyone living there is living under a harsh regime and one reason so many have decided to leave Syria and Iraq seeking a safer country to migrate to. In Iraq those that have connections to the Saddam regime are still given a hard time and they too have found themselves needing to leave Iraq to find safety. The war against Islamic State has displaced millions of people and caused a mass migration to Europe. Hopefully, long term with Islamic State gone some may decide to return home and help re-build the country. After all that is a big part of what the coalition is doing in Iraq, trying to make its people safe from tyranny and persecution.

The Landing Zone for the raid was in Deir ez-Zor governorate. From here we had to hike to their reconnaissance area close to the compound that Sayyaf was staying at. Once in a heavily camouflaged position. We used night vision goggles and a telescope to observe the target. We got into routine and began to feedback vital intelligence which would help us finalise the raid on Sayyaf. We monitored all movements into and out of the compound noting down exact timings and the numbers of 'tangos' or hostiles believed to be at the compound. The most important part was to ensure Sayyaf was at the location and we got Delta on the objective before he left the location.

With final preparations in hand a concise and detailed narrative of what each operator would do in order to complete their objective. The American's wanted Sayyaf alive if at all possible to see if they could get any intelligence from him. However, we all knew this was highly unlikely as these IS fighters loved to fight and by us killing them they believed they would become a martyr.

The American plan was for the compound to be strafed by F-18 Super Hornets to help soften the target and blow a hole in the side of the building before we moved in. Our other job was to help direct the F-18s onto their target as Delta made their way to the compound in helicopters carrying a total of fifteen Delta Operators, ready and armed to the teeth to get the job done. The adrenalin rush as you get close to the target is unreal. There's nothing else that gives you as much of an adrenalin rush as making assault by helicopter. The doors of the helicopter are sometimes open or taken off and you sit with your feet inside otherwise at full speed you would get yanked out of the. The whine of the rotors along with the roar of the engines as ground rushes below. There is a pounding rush of air pouring over you tugging at your clothes making you feel like a cavalryman on horseback heading into battle. You race towards the target at a relentless pace once that is still the most exhilarating part of an operation.

The actual raid was launched from Ain al Assad Air Base in Western Anbar Province with a flight time of one hour and fifteen minutes. The Iraqi government had been informed of the raid. The plan was for Pave Hawks to offload Delta close to the compound and cover their entrance with rockets and 7.62 miniguns to try to quell any resistance.

The first available F-18 dropped its payload which fell slightly short. A second F-18 repeated the bombing run and scored a direct hit.

The Pave Hawks flew in fast and low, which was the best way to avoid be caught by enemy radar. As the Pave Hawk slowed we slid our feet and legs over the edge of the chopper's floor ready to jump off as soon as we landed. I could just see a Delta operator hanging his head out the helicopter trying to see ahead through the dust kicked up by the helicopters rotors.

In our hide we could feel a cool breeze as we watched the assault go in from almost ringside seats. The night sky was full of stars and presented a beautiful sight. As it came in one Pave Hawk took a few rounds on the ground but was still able to carry on with the attack. Delta operator's moved forward as covertly as they could before all hell broke loose as the Pave Hawks opened up on the compound. Even with rockets and miniguns Delta was still taking fire and they had to fight their way forward. One Delta operator managed to hit an IS fighter firing his AK-47 straight at them. The IS fighter fell straight off the roof and hit the ground with a hollow thud. After entering the compound through the hole created by the F-18. Delta split up into teams and they all took different quarters of the large compound. It was a case of fighting through each and every room. For some Delta operators this meant hand to hand fighting. The hardest part as always is avoiding shooting any women and children which the Islamic State had decided to use as human shields. A so called 'double tap' to the head dropped any IS fighter found without any civilian loss. It was a scene of mayhem but not too dissimilar to a hostage rescue. A scenario the SAS and Delta has constantly trained for and is a big part of specials forces training.

The squad leader took the lead and pushed forward firing as they went. Even in the dark you could see the muzzle flashes from mainly AK-47s firing at them and then flashes from Delta weapons firing back in a much more controlled manner. I could also hear the distinctive sound of M16s being fired as well and assumed these were most likely IS fighters whom had taken possession of these American weapons from Iraqi forces.

Delta moved along the corridor which had doors on both sides. As they got just a few feet down the corridor an IS fighter suddenly appeared from behind a door. He was shot in the head and killed before he had time to lift his AK-47 up. Around the compound Delta operators were in a fierce firefight with IS fighters who fought tenaciously and were much better trained than we had expected. It was a slow raid by our standards. But, when you end up undertaking room by room clearance as well as searching for IEDs or booby traps it always slows down progress.

Finally, after hour an hour the compound was secure. When Sayyaf was found he tried to grab a handgun and he was shot in the chest twice. Delta had killed fifteen IS fighters, which included Sayyaf. The loss of Sayyaf would be a blow to Islamic State and another one of their key personnel taken out. As soon as the compound was secure we moved out of our hide to act as a cutoff for any IS fighters trying to flee. I am sure a few had fled the moment the Pave Hawks had opened up and Delta had begun their attack. In a couple of rooms, Delta found and captured Sayyaf's wife and rescued a Yazidi slave girl. This is another element of Islamic State I cannot understand. They sate they are religious but happily rape women and children. Forcing young girls into marriage. Tell me what religion allows that? I don't see Islamic State in any way as being religious. It is just an excuse to try to justify what they are doing. They are terrorists pure and simple who have no regard for human life. Many join from countries around the world for the excitement and promises of a good and opulent life at the expense of others. I think it is the excitement more than anything else that attracts young men to take up arms and fight for a terrorist organisation.

The operation had been successful. Along with spreadsheet information containing financial data. The Americans also recovered ancient Assyrian artefacts, ancient coins and other priceless artefacts. Along with a wealth of other useful intelligence materials, including mobile phones, laptops and documents. As Islamic State also operate heavily in cyber space, any account details, websites and cell numbers aid in tracking individuals and disrupting their operation. Islamic State are the first terrorists to be fighting a war online as well as on the ground. Global recruitment and communications is a key part of Islamic State indoctrination and radicalisation. They have made good use of the so called 'deep web' for communications and money transfer. Even using hard to detect bit coins which are electronic money to finance the purchase of weapons and ammunition including explosives.

Both the SAS and the UK government had not wanted our participation known about to ensure that potential political issues of British boots on the ground in Syria could be avoided. But, we had our cover blown by sources close to the Kurdish government who decided to disclose what role the SAS had played in the raid. I am sure the disclosure led to some form of personal gain on their part as well. As the media love Special Forces stories and the SAS have always been able to steal the headlines ever since the Libyan Embassy siege in London in 1984.

It was said after the raid that more information was obtained from the documents seized in the Sayyaf raid than from "any Special Forces operation in history." This was along with a large stockpile of cash due to the oil operation being largely cashed based. Captured spreadsheets retrieved in the raid showed that Islamic States total natural resource revenues in the six months between September 2014 and February 2015 amounted to about £190 million. Sayyaf's oil operation in the Deir Ezzour and al-Hasakah provinces in north-eastern Syria contributed to 72 percent of those revenues.

THREE - MISSION

To do the dangerous job we do means sacrifices, both physical and mental. Notwithstanding the long periods of time away from home and loved ones. I have a wife and a young son - it breaks my heart to leave them for such long periods. I miss seeing him grow up day by day and my wife at times feels like a single parent. There will come a time when I will no longer get sent off to foreign lands and get time to spend with my family. It is another life choice and I know it is a hard one for my family. They have the constant worry and fear of me being in harm's way. Retirement is still a few years away. But, I may choose to leave the regiment sooner. I am sure I will know exactly when the time had come for me to leave.

I'm no different to anyone else, I am no hero just a trained soldier. I just happen to have decided to fight for my country and in doing so found myself in some difficult situations. I get told how exciting it must be to be in the Army. I never tell anyone I am in the SAS, either just in the Parachute Regiment or Army. The less you say and the less exciting you make out your job to be the less questions you get asked. Those in the SAS never actually state they are in the SAS. Most of us, me included feel it is better to be the grey man. It keeps both yourself and your family much safer. Awkward situations are avoided and of course media attention which could lead to your cover being blown. As photos or news reports now navigate the world you never know what or how the information could be used. As they say what you put on the internet stays on the internet. Every keystroke picture or article read can now be tracked. ISIS actively search and use the internet for research on targets for their own intelligence. As a rule of thumb, I never say or do anything on the internet I not do in person in public as a civilian.

I don't personally see what I do as exciting. I feel it is more sheer terror than excitement at times. You never join the Army thinking you will become a killer or actually kill someone. Most of the lads join up for the challenge and be a part of something. The comradeship and brotherhood is another element that you won't find in any other occupation, where your life literally depends on the actions of another.

In Iraq we seemed to be getting a few more capture type raids. Intelligence would give us an individual and a location and we would go out and 'snag' them. Most of the time the raids we undertake go well. On the odd occasion it did not quite go according to plan. On one particular occasion I was coming back down off a rooftop after playing overwatch on a snatch operation. We had got in and out of the target in Iraq, without firing a round. As I got to the bottom of the stairs I heard the familiar sound of numerous AK-47s going off, followed by the more worrying call over the radio that we had a man down. The rest of the team were pinned down and trying to fire back. I ran down a side street trying to find a good spot to get up high. I heard an explosion as an IS fighter threw a grenade not too far from my location. I had no idea if it had been aimed at me or someone else. But, I was not going to hang about to find out. I climbed on a roof top across from where the firefight still raged. I quickly set up my DAN .338 rifle one fitted with a sound suppressor / flash hider. The DAN .338 sniper rifle is a new addition to the SAS. It is made by Israel Weapon Industries (IWI). The rifle is chambered for the powerful .338 Lapua Magnum cartridge. The DAN features a folding stock and lightweight aluminium alloy chassis. A long Picattiny rail runs along atop the receiver and forearm for mounting scopes and further set of forearm rails in the 3, 6 and 9 o'clock positions facilitate the mounting of bipods, laser devices, grips and other accessories. I got on with the business of hunting for a target. An IS fighter had just appeared with a belt fed weapon and he would be my first target. I got a shot straight through his head and saw the back of his skull blow off before he dropped like a stone to the floor. More IS fighters were coming down the street and I quickly fired a succession of rounds to halt them in their tracks. The rest of the team was still firing back, but still pinned down. I needed to get them some room to manoeuvre otherwise they were all screwed. Bullets were cracking through the air, some ricocheting off the walls in a series of small sparks. Matt and Chris started to get some serious fire down, knowing they were both outnumbered and outgunned. Matt knew he could not continue to stay in his current position and would need to move. The fighting continued as Matt and Chris ensured they conserved ammunition as they did not have a good line of sight on the enemy.

The other IS fighters were firing from round a corner and I could not get a good line of sight on them. My only option was to expose my position and move, literally jumping from one building to the next. Looking back, it was a silly thing to do. In the heat of battle, you have to make split second decisions. Sometimes good, sometimes bad - my gamble paid off and after landing badly with my Dan clattering to the ground. I quickly picked myself up and got into a position to fire.

I was just able to get the right hand side of one IS fighter in my crosshairs. I let off a round which sent the IS fighter's AK-47 flying into the air as he was pushed backwards by the force of the impact. Chris managed to hit another IS fighter in the shoulder. This was enough for the rest of the team to be able to get up and run at full pelt down the street with bullets nipping at their heels as they did so. I soon followed in hot pursuit. Before looping back to where the IS Commander was. He was dead, having been shot by his own fighters accidentally in the firefight. A bullet had ploughed completely into his leg, coming to rest just under the skin on the top of his thigh, missing the femur but hitting the femoral artery and he quickly bled to death. Other than grabbing his mobile phone he was left where he had fallen. I ran as fast as I could back to our rides. Almost leaping through the vehicle window throwing what I had collected onto the back seat before we sped off with rounds still impacting close by. Within a few minutes we were out of danger and could slow the pace down. We all took a deep breath and gave a sigh of relief. It had been a close call and we could have so easily been overrun. We had got out with just a few scratches from the odd small shrapnel wound.

Had it been a much larger force, equipped with heavier weapons it could have meant a very different outcome. You try not to dwell on the "what if" you focus on the outcome, do your job and get another successful operation under your belt. Sometimes operations go according to plan other times unforeseen events happen that completely change the plan you had. It requires a commander who can think on their feet and make decisions in real time while undertaking an assault to keep an operation a success.

FOUR – CLOSE SHAVE

We were 20 miles from Mosul. I stood up through the hatch of an Iraqi Humvee observing a small group of buildings when an RPG whizzed to my right. Everyone opened up including me on the .50 cal. The IS fighters responded with a few burst of fire but we kept the pressure on them with a large volume of fire. RPGs are not nice - especially when they burst as they shower the impact area with shrapnel. RPGs continued to be fired at us one after another. Whenever we saw the dust that flew up from where they were launched, we concentrated our fire on those locations.

Matt spotted a window from which some of the RPGs were being fired from. That soon had a large amount of rounds being pumped through the window. An RPG flew past just a couple of yards above my head. I dropped down into the Humvee just as it hit the ground and caused the vehicle to shudder from the blast wave. Chris let off a LAW and scored a direct hit. The rate of enemy fire suddenly dropped dramatically. Small arms fire was still flying around us along with the odd RPG. I spotted a building where enemy fire was coming from. I shouted to the rest of the team "Over there, large two storey building with four windows." I switched to my sniper rifle and while the lads got fire onto the positon. I lined my scope up ready to take a shot. I quickly set up for wind speed and distance. Just as I was about to fire, a blinding flash filled my scope as another RPG left the window. I could barely make out the outline of the figure holding the RPG but let off three rounds in quick succession. It was too dark inside the building to see if I had hit him or not. All I knew was that no more RPGs were fired from that window. The rest of the team moved forward to clear the buildings while I acted as overwatch from my Humvee. Rifle at the ready to take out any IS fighters who posed a threat or were trying to flee. The odd IS fighter was dropped by the lads as they entered one building. However, other than a couple of IS fighters found and killed inside. The threat had been neutralised and eight IS fighters lay dead across two buildings. Their bodies were searched for intelligence before we re-grouped, mounted up and headed towards the next village. In many ways the IS fighters did fight in a very similar way as the Taliban had in Afghanistan and much of what we learnt about the enemy there has been transferable. IS fighters like the Taliban wear no insignia so the usual sniper tactic of taking out a higher ranking officer is much harder unless you know exactly who they are.

The Taliban for instance did not like to stay still and shoot. They would much rather use flanking manoeuvres and engaged us with tactics that needed to be picked up early on. They knew we could bring down heavier firepower than they had. A quick ambush or setting numerous IEDs could yield better results for them. An IED was a good way to slow a convoy down, ambush it and kill as many British, American or coalition forces as they could. ISIS have not used quite the same tactics, but are very similar some having been through the same training camps. The Taliban like Islamic State found using mopeds or motorbikes a good way of getting about as was a harder target to locate and hit. On one occasion in Afghanistan, I remember nearing a small village a few miles away from Jalalabad going in for a typical 'snatch' raid on a Taliban commander. As we got close to the village we started to watch a local teenager on a moped who kept driving at speed across the front of us at a range of about 400 yards to the front of us. As soon as he came to a standstill I got my scope out to see if I could see what weapons if any he was carrying. Using a technique called 'baseline' a technique that has come from Israel. That states you look out for something that looks different to what you would expect to see. What you would normally expect to see is called the baseline. He stood out as he was the only local remaining in the area while the remainder of the locals were all heading away as quickly as possible.

We knew from experience he must be a Taliban spotter. We were very aware of this tactic having come across it before in Northern Ireland when we were fighting the IRA. In Northern Ireland these spies were given the nickname 'dickers' and we used the same term in Afghanistan for Taliban spies. The 'Dickers' or spies were usually unassuming civilians who would relay messages of the positions of British forces. The same happened in Afghanistan; these 'dickers' could be anything from children to tribal elders. They would use mobile phones, smoke, mirrors or even kites, which the Taliban had once banned, to report back the movement and strength of coalition forces. They got paid for any information they passed on.

Chris decided the best bet would be to give him a warning shot. As the moped approached us once again near to a junction. Chris fired a round from his C8 or L119A2 after being upgraded by Colt in 2013. The most distinctive new feature is the tan grip and buttstock.

The round whizzed past in front of the moped. The shock of the round caused the lad on it to nearly drop his moped on the floor catching it just in time. With that he got his moped upright jumped back on it and sped off into the distance, probably having had the fright of his life.

We finally reached the village and dismounted. I made my way to the roof of the tallest building to act as overwatch. The rest of the team made their way through meandering buildings. The village was eerily quiet. Although not that unusual as the occupants of villagers such as these would flee from the advancing Islamic State. Knowing all too well what they would do to the occupants especially the women and girls. The team continued to patrol through looking into doorways, but the whole village seemed completely deserted.

All of a sudden a shot rang out and everyone took cover by getting down low huddling into a couple of doorways. I swung my scope round to where the noise of the shot had come from and we all waited for further shots to come. There was obviously someone about and we had no idea if it was friend or foe. After a few minutes had passed with nothing further, the lads continued to push forward, only a little more cautiously now. As they turned a corner they were spotted by some malnourished dogs. All four of them were skin and bone with matted fur and looked in a pitiful state. They stood there snarling and growling a couple were foaming at the mouth. The team decided just to ignore them and carried on. Had one decided to attack it would have had to have been shot. The team finally made it to the far edge of the village and saw no one.

As they were about to turn round had head back a burst of gunfire flew over their head and they dropped to the ground rolling towards the side of the building to get into better cover. I had seen the muzzle flash from a small hill on the far side of the village. I waited for the IS fighter to pop back up so I could get a round into his head. I waited and waited but nothing happened. The rest of the team decided to crawl back down the way they had come from. I knew there had to be more IS fighters out there.

Just then my question was answered when an RPG came flying from over the hill and hit the area the SAS lads had just vacated. I still could not see anything and the rest of the team got some fire down as they retreated backwards. They decided to get themselves into a compound and onto the roof for a better vantage point. Once on the roof they began to fire off short bursts of fire at the hill. Hoping the IS fighter or fighters may pop out so I could get a shot off. Once again nothing happened and we waited for the next burst of fire or RPG.

The volley of fire finally came from our right flanks. The IS fighters had managed to move around unnoticed and get another burst of fire off at the rest of the team on the compound roof. The patrol opened up on the IS fighters position. Finally, I spotted a fighter in a group of trees to my far right. It seemed as if they were trying to circle us and attack from the rear flank.

My shot found its target hitting the fighter on the top of his head and blowing his head apart. We had no idea of strength, but that at least was one fighter out of the picture. It was a case of sitting, watching and waiting for someone to appear with another volley of fire.

We waited and waited and nothing happened. Rather than wait for a much larger Islamic State force to appear we decided the best idea was to get out of the village and move back into the desert.

Even as we mounted up there was nothing to be heard. Had we really been pinned down by a lone IS fighter or was the rest of the force waiting to ambush us? That is an answer we will never know. We mounted up and headed off back into the desert without hearing a further shot or seeing anyone else. The more IS fighters we could capture or kill would reduce their strength. If we could reduce their strength faster than they could recruit, we could turn the course of the war on Islamic State much quicker.

FIVE - SNIPER

I looked down the scope of my L115A3 bolt-action sniper rifle, with an effective range of 1500 metres. I could see all the way into the village, mothers scooped up their children and ran indoors. I felt like I was on the set of an old western movie when the bad guy comes to town. It was a typical Iraqi village made up of small and large compounds with dusty tracks instead of roads. To a westerner they looked so basic, but were functional and suited the climate very well. The streets were now deserted and a deathlike silence smothered the village. An SBS patrol was moving up onto a target compound on the edge of the village.

My job was to act as overwatch and protect the patrol. I had moved into position earlier on in the day slowly wilting under the hot sun. I was to take out any potential threat before it had a chance to kill any of the lads. ISIS could be sneaky and their tactics was to often lure coalition forces into an ambush or a trap. This was week four of my tour of duty in Iraq having come almost straight from another overseas operation. I was part of B Squadron, SAS mobility troop. Our job was to assist conventional forces in removal of various pockets of resistance and the targeting of key ISIS personnel.

I was two floors up on a compound roof with a commanding view of the main road into and out of the village. A light breeze whipped up small swirls of dust from the roof that kept on misting up the scope slightly. My radio burst into life to tell me the SBS patrol was approaching the edge of the village. I stared down my scope even more intensely watching for any movement which may turn into a threat. The SBS pickup's filled my scope as I followed them in. They screeched to a halt becoming enveloped in a large cloud of dust. Eight troopers leapt out.

They moved forwards hugging the sides of the buildings on a high state of alert looking for signs of IEDs and any potential threat. I trained my scope just ahead of them also looking for any potential threat. Almost out of nowhere a figure dressed in black appeared and raised his AK-47 directly at the advancing soldiers. His body now filled my crosshairs and I gently squeezed the trigger of my sniper rifle. I could feel the recoil from the weapon through my entire body as the rifle spat out a round. I had been holding my sights on the chest of the young male. I rocked back with the recoil, he disappeared from my crosshair. A killing shot drops a man so fast it seems like the earth just swallows him up. When I came back to rest again, the only hint that just an instant before a man had been standing there was a faint cloud of atomized blood and tissue momentarily suspended in the air.

The IS fighter lay dead, blood pouring out of what was left of his chest. This was my twelfth kill as a sniper. I cannot say I feel any real remorse or guilt. I try to see the enemy as a target that must be eliminated. If I don't take the individual holding a weapon or a bomb, then they will take either fellow soldiers or innocent people.

There is more to being a sniper than just being a good shot. The best shots are not necessarily the best snipers. Just because you can hit a target does not mean you can spot the target in the first place. I am not the best shot by a long way, but better than average at spotting a target. You have to be able to study your terrain and surroundings. In training you are taught to see things you previously missed such as discerning subtle shapes, noticing the smallest amount of movement. You have to train yourself to not only be an excellent observer but to keep your observation skills at the highest possible level.

The SBS continued forward. I took a deep breath realising I had saved them from being injured or killed. ISIS wanted all of us dead no matter what the cost was to them we were 'infidels.'

Out of the corner of my eye I noticed another black clad figure appear on the roof, this time he was carrying a RPG (Rocket Propelled Grenade) and about to fire. An RPG is designed to fragment into hundreds of shards of razor-sharp steel, which are blasted forward from the point of the explosion, fanning out and tearing flesh or light armour to shreds. RPG rounds can be set to either airburst mode going off after a set distance mid-air or explode on impact in detonating mode. The Taliban has used airburst mode to bring down helicopters by setting the RPGs to explode close enough for the shrapnel to shred hydraulic lines and electrical wiring looms.

I moved my crosshairs onto his central body mass, as I did so, rounds started to impact about ten feet from my location. They knew where I was – I was in as much danger as the SBS making their way up the street. I had to take out the RPG first and quickly move. I fired and the round found its target. The Taliban fighter was blown apart by the round. The RPG clattered to the ground next to the body parts of the deceased Taliban fighter.

I quickly packed up as yet another volley of fire hit the compound roof, as I slung rifle onto my back and picked up my C8. I made my way down the stairs of the compound and out onto the street. The butt of my C8 was pressed firmly into my shoulders and I pointed it in whatever direction I looked, seeking out any potential target. As soon as I had found a suitable location I radioed in a situation report and requested fire support. I could no longer see the eight man SBS patrol, but with IS fighters up high. A drone or fast jet was the best bet to locate and neutralize them.

Within minutes a single jet fighter was on station, its distinctive roar could be heard even when it was a couple of miles out. More than likely alerting the IS to its presence. It raced in and dropped a couple of bombs I had indicated which were away from the SBS patrol. The bombs landed throwing a bright orange flash and loud cloud of dust high into the sky.

The SBS had now made it into the village and were moving up onto their objective.

Finally, the patrol got to the compound and knocked on the door; there was no answer, so they kicked the door in. On entering, they found a family inside. A man along with his wife and three young children. As the team burst in the whole family started to scream and shriek. In the very few words of Pashto that one SBS lad knew he said that they were British soldiers and were not here to hurt them. They calmed down a little when one of the SBS lads offered the children some chocolate. The SBS knew IS fighters had been here but the family was too afraid of reprisals from the ISIS to say anything. The patrol still undertook a search of the compound but found nothing. This time ISIS had left without a trace and not left behind anything of any use.

They had obviously either fled before the SBS had arrived or found a new place to hide. More than likely using fear to force a villager to take them in. try and search each and every building would take a large amount of resources and do more harm than good. The mission was a partial success, we had picked up some local intelligence and killed another two IS fighters. The local commander we had hoped to capture had fled – which was a disappointment to us all. But, that was all part of the cat and mouse game we played with Islamic State.

SIX - PATROL

The term Jihad translates from Arabic as struggle. It is used to denote a religious duty of
Muslims. A person engaged in jihad is called a mujahid; the plural is mujahedeen. This term was used for the multi-national insurgent groups in Afghanistan fighting against the Soviet's occupation of Afghanistan from 1979 to the decision by the Soviets withdraw in 1989. The word jihad appears frequently in the Quran the religious text of Islam. The term Jihad within the Quran is often in the idiomatic expression "striving in the way of God." In Shia Islam Jihad is one of the ten Practices of the Religion. However, Jihad is often translated into "holy war." If military jihad is required to protect the Muslim faith against others, it can be performed using anything from legal, diplomatic and economic to political means. If there is no peaceful alternative, Islam also allows the use of force, but there are strict rules of engagement. Innocent people such as women, children, or invalids - must never be harmed, and any peaceful offers to stop any further bloodshed from the enemy must be accepted.

Military action is therefore only one means of jihad, and is very rare. To highlight this point, the Prophet Mohammed told his followers returning from a military campaign: *"This day we have returned from the minor jihad to the major jihad."* What he was saying was that on returning from armed combat in battle they would now be in the battle for self-control and betterment. If military action appears necessary, not everyone can declare jihad. A religious, military campaign has to be declared by a proper authority, advised by scholars, who say the religion and people are under threat and violence is imperative to defend them. The concept of "a just war" is very important.

The concept of jihad has been hijacked by many political and religious groups over the ages in a bid to justify various forms of violence. They have twisted and miss used the term to justify military action or various atrocities against innocent civilians. In most cases, Islamic splinter groups invoked jihad to fight against the established

Islamic order. Examples of sanctioned military jihad include the Muslims' defensive battles against the Crusaders in medieval times. Therefore, Islamic State are nothing more than a terror group using a twisted religious context to justify their actions.

Today, we were going back to check that IS fighters were not trying to re-infiltrate an area just to the north of Qayyarah, Iraq. After a larger Islamic State presence had been removed often a small number would try to infiltrate and become a nuisance. If needed, we would push them out once more. Islamic State has over the past twelve months began to feel the pressure with personnel losses and a reduction in funding. If Islamic State wanted to stick around, they would have to throw us out and push back the Iraqi forces.

We moved across a series of fields before stopping short of an intersection with a building on the corner and a few trees. Matt shouted "Over here." I dashed over along with Chris to find several bloody marks in the sandy ground followed by a series of drag marks. The IS fighters had dragged the wounded fighter along with them. Whoever it was, in a bad way judging from the blood loss.

In the current financial squeeze Islamic State was in. I would have not been surprised if they had been dragged away to have their organs harvested and sold on the black market before they died. One less IS fighter was not a bad thing no matter how callous that may sound. But, the atrocities and complete lack of humanity they had shown to fellow countrymen made you feel that way towards them.

We continued to patrol forwards as the temperature soared into the high 30s. We came across a mosque that had a series of heavy padlocks on all the doors and windows. It was more than likely an Islamic State staging post. We were not permitted to enter unless we had seen enemy activity inside. It would be far better politically and religiously to get the Iraqi Army to check it out. We could call in an air strike but again that could cause political issues locally. Part of fighting a war in another country is to try and not cause issues with the local populous. The British Army call it "winning the hearts and minds" and to be honest it does make sense. It was exactly the same during my tours in Afghanistan where over time you could get locals to trust you and be almost happy to have soldier's there to stop the Taliban returning and make them feel safe once again.

We continued on patrol for the next five hours moving around the area we had just cleared. Thankfully, we found no sign of Islamic State other than some historical statues that they had purposely torn down. A couple of looted shops and a police station where all the weapons and vehicles had been taken. By now we had just about adapted to the heat and instead of sweating all the time we only sweated when running or wearing our helmets. You still had to hydrate regularly as becoming dehydrated not only slowed you down but could end up making you feel quite ill with headaches, tiredness and even nausea. The other part of patrolling was the concentration and keeping completely aware of your surroundings at all times. Making sure all your arcs were covered. This was very draining in itself without the added extra concern of IEDs, booby traps or mines left as a pleasant surprise for forces re-entering areas once held by Islamic State. Although it was not to the same level as what the Taliban undertook in Afghanistan. The smallest amount of soil out of place or strangely placed boulders could indicate an IED. One of the Russian legacies from their occupation of Afghanistan was the large numbers of mines behind. The Taliban made good use of this free resource and would dig them up. Often stacking two or three mines on top of each other. These would still go off under the weight of a man pretty much blowing them into hundreds of pieces. But their real use was against the various convoys carrying men and equipment around Afghanistan. One big reason it was safer for troops to be moved around in choppers during the war.

In one small deserted village we climbed onto the roof of a small apartment block three stories high. The stairway was lined with windows which led to an open roof and a good vantage point. In the almost quiet stillness you could almost forget you were in a warzone with danger just around the corner. Parts of Iraq are truly stunning. Something I had not really appreciated until those few moments standing on the apartment roof. I won't say it quite had the same rugged beauty as parts of Afghanistan. Especially the awesome mountainous backdrop on the Afghanistan/Pakistan border. I could see across the village and into the wilderness of the desert. We did not have time to dwell though as you never knew who might be watching us. Standing up there we were sitting ducks for an Islamic State sniper to chalk up another hit.

We made our way back to our vehicles and sped off as dusk fell to the most intense and beautiful display of yellow and orange hues as the sun set. I have never seen a sunset like it before. Iraq like Afghanistan is full of surprises some good and some not so good. But I have grown fond of Iraq during my time here.

SEVEN – PESH HELP

At around 0100 hours, we found our target between Sinjar and Mosul. We were about half a mile away as we sat and observed the IS fighters. We slowly circled their position taking notes and observing their movements through our night vision goggles. As dawn approached we found a rocky outcrop to hide in and conceal ourselves until nightfall. For the next week we would be nocturnal operating at night and sleeping during the day. There was just the four of us including myself on this operation – Andy, Chris and Kev. I was the second longest serving operator in the group. Andy having two more years' service than me. Chris was the baby on his second year of service.

Chris was over five feet six inches tall and sported a thick goatee. He had already provided himself to be up there with the best. He was a true twenty first century soldier with an array of technical skills I could only dream of. He originally joined the Royal Signals before moving to the Parachute Regiment and passing selection for the SAS. His physical ability meant he got through the physical side with ease. It was like he had been born to be in the SAS. He was already a crack shot when he joined the unit. But, was now even better. He knew the firing ranges, velocity and trajectory of every weapon the SAS used. He took some stick though for making the rest of us look bad.

After resting throughout the day we packed up and as soon as it was dark moved off into the night. We estimated we had a three to four-hour trek to our next reconnaissance point. The final mile to our objective involved crossing an Iraqi motorway. We were deep inside an Islamic State controlled area. They would more than likely have patrols on the motorway. The area we had entered was a hive of activity, with various Islamic Sate patrols going up and down the motorway, randomly stopping vehicles and checking its occupants. If caught, we would be paraded on television before promptly being executed. The propaganda victory for Islamic State would be second to none, even if it caused further world outrage.

The motorway was not going to be an easy task to cross. Using a bridge would make us completely overt and even crossing the motorway we ran the risk of being spotted. Our best bet was to travel alongside the motorway and cross at the darkest point to minimise the chance of being seen.

We ended up yomping several miles to find a safe crossing point. We still had a deep culvert and the motorway itself to navigate across one by one to reduce being seen. Once across motorway they were not that far from the enemy base we needed to gather intelligence on prior to a combined attack with the Kurdish Army. The base was full of activity with trucks containing IS fighters entering and quite soon afterwards leaving the base. We spent a couple of hours observing the base. Before deciding we needed to get back across the motorway before first light. The raid was to go in and destroy the base and gather as much intelligence as we could. If we could seize a commander's mobile phone or laptop we could gather further details on Islamic State members to fulfil the need for an accurate picture to aid in bombing missions and track key Islamic State personnel.

We made it back across the motorway as dawn broke, thankfully being a Sunday morning there was hardly any traffic. Which aided us getting across undetected and back into cover during daylight hours.

After a further forty-eight hours we made it back to base and began the usual planning and final orders and intelligence prior to the mission. The Peshmerga soldiers were used mainly as backup and fire support. Experience had taught us that their haphazard technique of spraying bullets in all directions could lead to vital intelligence being lost. I knew my role in the assault as the sniper was to take out sentries and cover the troop and Peshmerga as they assaulted the base.

The plan of attack was to be dropped in by helicopter about a mile of the mission. SAS troopers would be in front with the Kurds at the rear finishing off and cutting off any fleeing IS fighters. The gates to the base would be breeched with a single LAW fired by Chris. I had found a small hill about a quarter of a mile away to set up my snipper rifle and associate kit. I had a spotter with me as well to help with ranges and wind direction.

It was not long before the rest of the team had hit the main entrance road and began to move down it, staying low. Further along, they moved behind a small escarpment that ran alongside the road. The base was surrounded by a wall, behind which there could be a second perimeter fence. After doing a final recce on the objective, it became clear that there were quite a few vehicles, that looked like Toyota Hiluxs, some with weapons, possibly a DSHKs and .50 cal mounted on them along with other IS fighters milling about some carrying RPDs. The Peshmerga's would be on our left flank giving us fire support. The night time sky was darker than normal further aiding us in getting up close to the base unnoticed. We made the assumption that the IS would not think to use night vision goggles, even if they possessed any. Their tactics and the way they fought was almost identical to al-Qaeda having attended the same training camps. Some IS fighters had fought in Afghanistan as well gathering vital knowledge on how U.S. and other forces operated. Chris got his LAW out and fired it. Blowing the entrance gates off in the process. These massive gates must have gone some twenty feet up in the air before crashing down just missing the IS fighters trying to avoid them.

The initial assault was textbook and IS fighters were initially surprised by the attack. This surprise soon turned to anger and repelling us at all costs. I quickly picked off a couple of IS fighters located on roof tops close to the entrance to the base. The SAS troopers pushed forward, before noticing a pile of sandbags in a corner that looked like an enemy position. This position was empty, so they continued forward another fifty feet. A group of IS fighters all brandishing an AK-47. A couple of them had RPG-7, RPGs. Were currently hiding down the side of an old Iraqi Army truck.

The SAS troopers managed to dive behind a wall just in time. An American Humvee approached. It was funny as well as a little disconcerting to see an American Humvee driving around complete with a US M240B machine gun mounted on top. The M240B was deadly, firing around 750 -950 7.62 rounds a minute and just over a one mile effective range. Islamic State had managed to capture many American vehicles including M1 Abrahams tanks. Their biggest issue was getting parts to keep them serviceable. The U.S. Governments job has been to ensure Islamic State could not get their hands on any parts.

The Peshmerga fire support team got into position. The darkness seemed to have enveloped everything except what was in front of me. As I watched intently through my cross hairs. My mind became focused on the mission, blocking out everything else. Small arms fire had opened up and become quite effective. This was followed by a 12.7mm DShK. These Russian anti-aircraft guns could churn out 600 rounds per minute. It made a highly effective ground attack weapon that could shred lightly armoured vehicles, tearing through walls and even trees. Tracer rounds were now whizzing across the sky, bringing some limited light to the gloom, before ricocheting or impacting the ground. The SAS troopers were in a full on firefight. Even if some of the IS fighters had no idea which way they should be firing

Small arms fire was now coming from all directions as they drew closer to the main building. It was still wildly inaccurate, but it must not be forgotten that the AK-47 is only really accurate to about 50 yards, it is much better at putting plenty of rounds down with good short range stopping power. Some IS fighters are very good at what they do; however, the majority are poor shots having only received very basic training. It is their tenacity and will to fight to the death that makes them such a danger. At times like the Taliban, I am positive they have been high on drugs and continued to advance even with quite serious injuries.

One of the lads managed to get a couple of rounds into a DShK gunner. The rounds hit the gunner side on, pushing him slightly side wards before he slumped forward over the DShK, and for an instant it fell silent. But a split second later a second fighter had climbed onto the weapon, and the DShKs gaping muzzle began spitting fire in our direction once more.

Once inside the main building, an assault team had been allocated a floor. My job switched to preventing anyone else entering the building almost acting as flank protection. A fierce firefight raged on inside the building as the rest of the SAS troop overwhelmed and killed everyone inside the building. Picking up any worthwhile intelligence as they went. Bodies were checked for mobile phones and anything else of use. We had a small window of time as Islamic State reinforcements would have been alerted the moment we began our assault. Some reinforcements had begun to arrive as we made our escape.

It was going to be a slow fighting retreat as thousands of rounds buzzed all round us as more IS fighters seem to pop up, almost as if they had been buried in the ground and we were in the midst of some form of zombie apocalypse. The Peshmerga continued to offer fire support, but our own fire support needed to pull back as well, with us giving them covering fire, as they made a hasty retreat back to our evacuation point. I managed to take out a couple of IS fighters as we made our fighting retreat. Before they gave up and let us flee into the night, possibly hoping another patrol my find us and finish us off. The mission was considered a success. We had gathered up highly useful intelligence that would be useful for planning and coordination of further attacks. It would also aid us in the training of Peshmerga, giving them valuable insight and intelligence into Islamic State to aid in planning further operations and raids. The base was obliterated by a couple of bombs from RAF Typhoon jets so they could not be re-occupied by them.

EIGHT - SUPPORT

We continued to work with the Iraqi Army; our missions typically would take us ahead of their main advance scouting for positions and enemy strongholds. Often to get to these strongholds we had to fight or go around 'friction points.' We knew Islamic State had a few positions in the area of Tikrit. While Islamic State had a stronghold in and around Mosul and towards Baiji they still only really had thin strips of land. The areas they operated in however was much larger, simply due to the size of Iraq. Between 2014 and 2016 Islamic State has lost around 40% of the populated territory it once had in Iraq. Air strikes alone have killed an estimated 25,000 IS fighters in Syria and Iraq. Six hundred of those in the first three months of 2016. This has cut Islamic States strength in half; but it is not just the number of fighters which have been cut but also its finance stream from selling oil on the black market. At its peak Islamic State was estimated to be earning £1 million a day from selling oil alone. With repeated airstrikes on oilfields this funding stream has been reduced by a third. Such is the financial impact that IS fighters had their salaries cut in half to £120 to £500 a day depending on rank. It is believed that Islamic State only has around 30,000 fighters. They are even removing organs from injured IS fighters to sell on the black market to help raise funds. The large profits Islamic State made from oil was the main reason it was decided to target Islamic States oil infrastructure with air strikes. By reducing Islamic States ability to produce oil and profitability has in reduced income. Even after 30 percent of the oil infrastructure had been destroyed Islamic State was still making not far off £1 million a day from the sale of crude oil. Islamic State maintains its oil production by offering handsome salaries to skilled oil workers. These workers earn at least three times the average Syrian salary of £35 per month for an accountant. This goes up to eight times the average salary per month for a drilling technician.

Islamic State at one point was able to easily get new recruits from around the world not just for oil production but the foot soldiers required to attack and hold territory. The recruits were able to pour into Iraq and Syria using a wide open stretch of rugged border. This stretch became known as the 'Gateway to Jihad'. An example of one border crossing not far from Reyhanli, Turkey is just a dry, dusty track that snakes its way up to and across the border from Turkey into Syria. It is one of the ancient smuggling routes crisscrossing over the hills to Syria, the border is marked by nothing more than the odd scraps of barbed wire. The path leads down to the Orontes River, which meanders through the valley of olive plantations, and on the other side is Syria. This where an alarmingly easy route to enter Syria. Border guards would even turn a blind eye for as little as £7 or $10. It was estimated that at its peak around 20 foreign recruits were travelling through it each day on this poorly policed border area, of mountain passes and plains without confronting security. Once in eastern Turkey, recruits hook up with Islamic State handlers and embark on spending sprees in local army equipment shops. They could buy hunting knives, sniper rifle sights, binoculars and desert camouflage fatigues. There is an example of one IS fighter who walked into a shop waving $50,000 in bundles of cash as he bought a thousand 'magazine vests' for carrying spare AK-47 rifle ammunition clips. Turkey was initially reluctant to stop anyone from crossing. Allowing weapons and supplies destined for recognised Syrian opposition groups to cross. Although, this flow of new recruits has been reduced dramatically since Turkey tightened its border security succumbing to European and U.S. pressure. It has helped control the number of new recruits replenishing those that have been lost. A steady ramping up of military operations in Iraq will only see their numbers drop further. More boots on the ground are to be sent along with Apache helicopters, which more than proved there worth in Afghanistan and both Iraq wars.

  On Monday 21 April 2016, B-52 bombers were used for the first time to carry out a bombing mission on Islamic State weapons storage facility near the town Qayyarah, Iraq. The B-52s had not long arrived at Al Udeid Air Base in Qatar before being deployed replacing B-1B

Lancer bombers as the primary bomber in Syria and Iraq. The B-52 can carry a mighty payload and has proven its destructive power with its ability to destroy vast swaths of rain forest during the Vietnam War.

The prize for Islamic State was Baghdad with IS units being sent in to wreak havoc. Although the number has dwindled over the past twelve months and has Islamic State are slowly pushed out of Iraq will become much less of an issue. More often than not any attack on Baghdad has been foiled. They have been taken out before their assault could begin with an airstrike. Islamic State has not been able to mount a successful offensive operation since Ramadi and Palmyra in May 2015. Moreover, whenever it has tried, the attack has been smashed quickly and efficiently; typically suffering 60 percent or higher casualties than is was previously. Islamic State in its current state is like a boxer in the final rounds of a fight who won't go on for much long before they are knocked out. Although, they will get back up and continue to be a problem for some time to come. Training harder and trying again to take a swing at various countries. With more terrorist attacks on individual nations in an attempt to bring governments to accept their demands.

However, even if pushed out of Syria and Iraq they will move to a new area such as Libya. They will continue to indoctrinate and radicalise young minds around the world. They will continue to mount terrorist attacks such as the ones in Paris and Brussels. All the world can do is be vigilant and try to stamp out the radicalisation in the first place. Religious communities have their part to play in making sure concerns over individuals are passed onto the authorities. Those at danger of being radicalised are supported by their community and not given a reason to be radicalised in the first place.

We darted around Iraq as two troops totalling sixteen men to take on any stronger resistance we came across. On one occasions we were coming towards an IS base when a patrol outside the perimeter spotted us. The firefight started off as the odd pot shot but quickly ratcheted up as IS fighters seemed to come pouring in from all directions. This was one hell of a firefight with rounds flying around in all directions. I stared to take down IS fighter after IS fighter with my C8 assault rifle. It was like playing a video game with the enemy re-spawning. We called in for air support, but that was going to be delayed. The firefight lasted for a couple of hours, with the fire seeming to die down for a while before stoking up again. In most firefights it would last for maybe a few minutes to maybe an hour depending on the numbers of fighters we were engaging. This firefight just seemed to go on and on. They were steadily advancing on our position and if air support did make it to us we would get caught in the blast. We had no choice but to make a fighting retreat, just as we thought, "shit, we are going to die if don't escape" a pair of F-18s came rolling in and dropped a couple of bombs right in the middle of the IS fighters. The explosion ripped through them. I saw arms, leg and other body parts flying off in all directions as a giant yellow and orange plume stretched out into the sky. The amount of dust caused by the explosion virtually blinded us. As the dust settled other than the odd bit of sporadic fire, air support had saved our butts big time.

   We used the explosion to make good our escape and returned back to base to a gleeful head shed. Not because we had won, but because we had made it all back alive and he did not want to lose any one. When soldier's start to die especially lots of them, public opinion starts to change. You only have to look at Vietnam and to a much lesser extent Afghanistan. The big reason there are not more boots on the ground is down to politics more than anything else.

   I am not embarrassed to say, I love my country. In the wake of Brexit we are should all be proud to be British and embrace all cultures and nationalities who live in the UK. The country has been and will continue to go through turmoil as terrorists try to cause issues. As we leave the EU and walk a different path. The one thing we must not do is end up fighting each other over issues that really do not matter. The most important part, is as a nation stick with our amazing tolerance and work together as a nation.

We do still have a great nation and the national anthem still gives me a twinge of proud. I know I am in pretty much the best Special Forces unit in the world with some of the most highly trained specials forces people in the world. The SAS and David Stirling are very British in their innovative and different approach to a problem. Britain has always been on the side of those that needed help and support within the world. Our role in the SAS has been to stamp out terrorism and bring to justice those that have committed atrocities. Along, with protecting innocent people and gathering intelligence from the various radical groups around the world that wants to try and harm the currently frail world stability. We are a surgical tool and have been used wisely over the years, even more so since 9/11.

NINE – SHADER

Islamic State is the greatest terrorist threat the world has ever known. These individuals are totally insane, their indoctrinated self-belief means they do not fear death, merely embrace it. They think nothing of killing anyone who will not follow their way of life. They will even kill their own if they do not toe the line or dare to speak out. Islamic State, like al-Qaeda, are classed as an Islamic fundamentalist group with Islamic fundamentalist beliefs and goals. They are advocates of the return of Muslims to the fundamental tenets of Islam, calls for the liberation of Muslims through the return to pure Islam and the creation of an Islamic state, called the caliphate. Islamic State sees pure Islam and an Islamic State as the only way to get rid of the problems faced by Muslims around the world.

Islamic State emerged from radical Sunni jihadists in Iraq who fought under the banner "al-Qaeda in Iraq." Since 2004 their goal has been to create a caliphate - a hard line Islamic state crossing over the borders of Syria and Iraq. The single most important factor in Islamic State's rapid expansion has been the conflict between Iraqi Shias and Iraqi Sunnis. The majority of Iraqis are Shias. However ex-dictator Saddam Hussein was a Sunni and the absolute power of his Ba'ath party gave Sunnis the belief that they are the real majority and legitimate rulers. The difference between the two largest Muslim groups originated with a controversy over who got to take power after the Prophet Muhammad's death in 632AD. Abu Bakr was chosen as caliph, but a minority of Muslims favoured another man, Ali. Ali's followers became known as Shiat Ali, partisans of Ali – Shias. In 656, Ali became the fourth caliph after Abu Bakr was assassinated. Some Muslims, the ancestors of today's Sunnis, rebelled against him. Ali himself was assassinated in 661 after violence spread.

Islamic State have also been called ISIL (Islamic State of Iraq and the Levant) and ISIS (Islamic State of Iraq and Syria). Then on June 29, 2014, Islamic State announced the establishment of a new caliphate - meaning succession, and the group formally changed its name to Islamic State, often referred to as IS. Islamic State have a self-proclaimed status for religious authority over all Muslims across the world. They wish to bring Muslim inhabited regions around the world under its political control and sharia law. Starting with Iraq, Syria and territory in the Levant region. Which includes Jordan, Israel, Palestine, Lebanon, Cyprus and an area in southern Turkey including Hatay.

In 2012, sensing an opportunity, Abu Bakr al-Baghdadi Islamic State's leader dispatched some foot soldiers to join the fighting against Bashar al-Assad's government in Syria. In 2013, he announced that the group was merging with Jabhat al-Nusra, the other al-Qaida affiliate in Syria, to form a new group called the Islamic State in Iraq and al-Sham. Nusra, predominantly Syrian in membership, is more focused on the overthrow of Assad, whereas Islamic State is more international and interested in expanding its territory and enforcing Sharia law. Abu Bakr al-Baghdadi is our current top target and remains quite elusive and a high priority target.

This was not the first time the SAS had been to Iraq, operators had taken part in both of the Gulf Wars and the subsequent search for Saddam Hussein. The first Gulf War saw the SAS hunting down Scud missiles alongside Delta in an area of operations called Scud Alley. The second Gulf War was the liberation of Iraq and the subsequent hunt for the leaders of the Saddam Hussein regime. We were also there to aid Iraqi forces in the quelling of terrorist forces trying to wrangle control of parts of Iraq.

Some of the lads I was with, like myself had been to Iraq before and they would prove good sources of intelligence. Their knowledge of not only the terrain but the local people would help greatly. The SAS has been back in Iraq along with the SBS, Delta and SEALs since 2014. With the odd mission which has seen Special Forces 'popping' into Syria and more recently Libya. Syrian and Libyan missions are still kept top secret for fear of political repercussions. In Iraq we have helped to train up the Iraqi Army, undertake surveillance and even perform the odd takedown mission. Snipers like me have been heavily used to take out key personnel at a distance.

Islamic State is well equipped with the usual DShK-38 12.7mm heavy machine guns, various mortar tubes, RPGs, PKMs and AK-47s. On top of these various American weapons including the M-16 have been captured from Iraqi forces as they advanced through Iraq. They have even captured the formidable M1 Abrahams tank. Although, Islamic State, don't have the technical knowhow nor parts to service them. They have been destroyed by us once located.

On our arrival in Iraq in December 2015, we were quickly deployed and I found myself and the rest of my patrol driving around in Toyota Hilux's or other civilian trucks due to blending in well to local vehicles and standing out less than some of the military vehicles we have used. We would wear jeans or local Arab dress so as not to bring attention to ourselves and fit the vehicles with special markers which identify them to Coalition aircraft in order that they are not shot at.

We drove through the desert until we came upon an Iraqi Army base and rested there for a couple of hours before setting off again. We were headed towards the area around Mosul an Islamic State stronghold. Amongst the long stretches of wilderness, there was also small towns and settlements dotted around. We decided to skirt round them rather than go through. Observing what was going on. Our mission was to locate where enemy strongpoints were and make a note of locations and enemy strength. Any high ground we found offered us a more commanding view to survey a larger area. Islamic State did send out the odd patrol but they were more focused on trying to keep what they had while trying to creeping forwards further into Iraq. We had neither the ammunition nor the firepower to get into a large scale firefight. But, we had enough ammunition to protect ourselves.

We had one contact during our day's operation when some IS fighters started to engage us from about 200 yards away. Evil green tracer rounds tore up the ground in front of us. I fired the .50 cal changing to the 60 as we sped off into the desert. By the end of the day we had travelled hundreds of miles and picked out various Islamic State bases and strongholds. We rested up for a few hours until nightfall before heading back to our operations base and the usual debrief as to what we had seen. This would be passed on to the intelligence services and Iraqi Security forces to aid in their operations. Our job was to help train and support and even accompany the Peshmerga on various operations. Peshmerga means "one who confronts death" or "one who faces death". "Pesh" means to stand in front of while "merga" means death.

Our specialist skills were still required though. Either for hostage rescue or capturing a key figure the Pesh would be used as fire support, if used at all depending on the mission. I like the other operators preferred taking Islamic State head on, one on one. Although we felt they were a dumbass group. Islamic State should never be underestimated their resolve and tenacity is second to none. Their weakness is blind faith and lack of training in some areas.

It was dark by the time we made it across the torturous desert and onto an asphalt road which enabled us to pick up the pace and head home avoiding any form of contact.

Once back at base we went through the usual debrief. These often have a mixture of intelligence agency personnel and Special Forces personnel. Including intelligence analysts, GCHQ personnel and anyone else invoked in the operation including air support if they had been involved.

The debrief was linked to our after action report. We use the debrief to identify what went well and what went wrong. Also looking at points to improve on as every operation is considered a learning opportunity. Then it was time for some grub and getting our heads down for some sleep before the next operation.

A week later an eight-man patrol found ourselves in an immense firefight just outside a small settlement that had around fifteen IS fighters occupying it. Once they opened up they never seemed to stop. A small wall next to my head exploded in a cloud of dust and debris as a steady stream of bullets flew just a few inches above my head. I lay flat on the ground returning fire as best as I could with my C8. I started to crawl as fast as I could, eventually reaching better cover where I could get a better rate of fire down directly onto the advancing IS fighters. We fought them for a couple of hours and as dawn broke their guns fell silent. We had killed twelve, one lay wounded and two had decided to flee. We all slumped down outside our backs propped up on a brick wall. Exhausted and battle weary with a few superficial cuts and nicks we had survived. These Islamic State nutters could fight. What must be realised is that Islamic State wants to engage troops on the ground. The recent attacks have been to try and force countries to deploy troops by causing a massive outcry. It is as if they have something to prove not just to themselves but to the whole world that they can take on the west. Such is their self-belief - they are sure they would win as well. However, as the war against Islamic State has gathered momentum and the coalition has not just reduced Islamic State numbers but gradually pushed them back and areas have successfully been reclaimed. This has had the effect of encouraging more and more Sunni tribesmen to abandon Islamic State or encourage them to defy Islamic State by joining Sunni Mobilization Forces such as Hashd ash-Shaabi. Iraqi high command is still a bit of a problem but again coalition forces have helped train and prove that Iraqi forces can successfully take on Islamic State. This has also helped the coalition to have a greater say in which Iraqi commands are entrusted to lead key ground operations. However, the Iraqi Army has been partly rebuilt, and those units retrained and re-equipped by the coalition are performing noticeably better than the others. While the coalition's military power is slowly building, the increasing pressure on Islamic State is diminishing its capacity to resist.

TEN - TECH

The Osprey lifted off into the night sky. In the rear it carried an American M1161 Growler Light Strike Vehicle (LSV). These compact and lightweight (two tonne) vehicles have minimal ballistic or blast protection. They are powered by a 2.8 litre four-cylinder diesel with 132bhp with a top speed of 85 mph on a road. They are designed to be able to go off-road to avoid mines and IEDs. They are a step up from the DPVs we have also used. I was already sitting in the driver's seat of the Growler as we came into land. The ramp dropped and I hit the Gas speeding off into the night. I hit a soft patch and the Growler veered to the right, I had to put in opposite lock to carry on going forward. The other two Growlers started to check in over the radio and we regrouped about a mile away from the landing zone. We had an area of operations to again go in and perform recognisance. Some of this was to be done by eyeball and some of it was to be undertaken by drones in the form of the PD-100 Black Hornet. The PD-100 UAV itself is 10 × 2.5 cm and weighs 16g. It can fly for around 20 minutes with a classified range. It takes about 20 minutes to learn ow to fly it. We first used these in Afghanistan. By 2013 we had 324 in service. U.S. Forces started testing them in March 2015. They are currently testing an upgraded version of the PD-100 to see how they get on. Marines Special Operations have also been testing the PD-100. It is a good piece of kit even if the actual helicopter looks a bit like a toy. You control the UAV with a joystick with several buttons and what is best described as a tablet which gives a live feed of what the UAV is seeing. Control of the drone is semi-automatic via movement buttons. GPS is used to locate enemy positions or items of interest; these can be used for airstrikes or to plan how an attack will be undertaken. It is fitted with three cameras and the latest Black Hornet has both long-wave infrared and day video sensors that can transmit video streams or high-resolution still images via a digital data-link with a 1-mile range.

"Black Hornet is a game-changing piece of kit. Previously we would have sent soldiers forward to see if there were any enemy

fighters hiding inside a set of buildings. Now we are deploying Black Hornet to look inside compounds and to clear a route through enemy-held spaces. It has worked very well and the pictures it delivers back to the monitor are really clear. And Black Hornet is so small and quiet that the locals can't see or hear it.
British Army Major Adam Foden

We continued our drive into the desert looking for a suitable place to hide before dawn broke. We chose and area away from where Islamic State were known to be operating. Although that would not mean we could not be detected by a patrol. Although, it was rare for them to venture so deep into the desert. They much preferred to stay close to their territory and repel attacks from ourselves or Iraqi forces.

Islamic State has been described as one of the richest militant groups in the world. In June 2014, when the group took over the city of Mosul, Islamic State reportedly plundered a government vault at the Mosul Central Bank, taking millions in state money (high estimates place the total amount the group looted as £1 billion). It has seized oil fields in Syria and Iraq and is allegedly making significant money selling Syrian and Iraqi crude on the black market; most recently, France has accused the Syrian regime of Bashar Assad of purchasing its own oil from Islamic State. Additionally, it has been reported that Islamic State makes millions through kidnapping and ransoms, involvement in the smuggling and underground trade of stolen Iraqi antiquities, and extortion in the areas it has conquered.

Islamic State have become masters of using social media as a weapon. In previous times, advancing armies smoothed their path with bombardments or missiles before launching an attack. Islamic State instead made use of social media to achieve the same result with tweets and a movie. This social media propaganda worked in Mosul where Iraqi soldiers fled their posts. It was thought that thirty-thousand Iraqi troops fled in terror from 800 IS fighters. They feared they would face a gruesome fate if they were captured by IS fighters in uniform.

Islamic State has made use of an app called the Dawn of Glad Tidings. This app has allowed Islamic State to use their accounts to send out centrally written updates. Released simultaneously, the messages swamp social media, giving Islamic State a far larger online reach than their own accounts would otherwise allow. The Dawn app pumps out news of the terror group's advances, gory images, or frightening videos like Swords IV – creating the impression of an uncontrollable and unstoppable force. All of this propaganda is designed to put fear into their enemies at the same time aiding in moral of IS fighters.

The next day we were given orders via our Satcom to clear a building a few miles away to our south. A local commander was doing his 'rounds.' Our job was to take him out. We decided to go in on foot for the last mile concealing our rides behind a large sand dune. We had 'glassed' the target to look for suitable entrance points and further intelligence. A Predator drone was going to aid us as our eye in the sky, courtesy of the CIA.

The MQ-1 Predator was originally conceived in the early 1990s for aerial reconnaissance and forward observation roles. It carries a variety of cameras and other sensors. It is also able to carry and fire two AGM-114 Hellfire missiles or other munitions. The war against Islamic State has seen their retirement pushed from 2015 to 2018.

It may not look sequenced but the SAS sweep through a building almost effortlessly. This is where our extensive amount of time in the' killing house' at Hereford, pays off with each operator knowing instinctively how to flow as a team. This includes being able to place two shots into an eye socket at 50 feet – known as the "double tap." To those being assaulted they often only see dark figures behind the flash form the flash bangs before meeting their maker.

It only took a matter of minutes to get the PD-100 UAV ready to go before I held it up and launched it from my hand, flying towards a potential Islamic State position, the idea was to fly in and observe the area around, looking at strength and enemy armour which Islamic State had at his location. We also wanted to get eyes on the main target and look for a suitable assault point. Marc flew the PD-100 in and it quickly found a couple of BMPs which Matt clicked on the screen to get their GPS co-ordinates which could be used for a bombing run/ The PD-100 UAV quickly made it over the area to be recce'd, before starting a further sweep and picking up twenty Islamic State fighters and a single T-72. It looked un-operational but its co-ordinates were also taken. It was time to bring the PD-100 in and pass on our intelligence and co-ordinates. These were quickly passed onto a pair of RAF GR4 Tornado jets which had been diverted from another fire support mission. As the Tornado jets made their way towards the target area. A Predator drone loitering in the area would be brought in to assess the damage and follow our assault.

With the enemy armour destroyed it was our turn to go in and take the local commander out. It would have been great f I could have just taken him out with a sniper round. But, Islamic State had realized that they needed to better protect key figures from potential sniper fire. After successful operations by the SAS and other special forces at taking out key personnel at long range. We kept low and moved at speed towards our objective. It was a case of simply following the acrid black smoke emanating from the various vehicles that had been obliterated by a handful of bombs. We faced no resistance as we made it inside the compound. As soon as we stepped inside small arms fire opened up sending chunks of the compound walk flying off in all directions. One small chunk bouncing off my lightweight Kevlar helmet.

Instinctively we hunted for a target and Chris quickly did a double tap before we pushed forward sliding along the walls and clearing each room. We found no further resistance and other than a couple of females who were secured and later turned out to be Kurdish sex slaves. There was no one else in the building. Mobile phones and any other intelligence was secured. Before, we made our way back out and into the relative safety of the desert.

It would later turn out the IS commander had been burnt to a crisp in the BMP he had decided to hide in to escape sniper fire. He had been tipped off that an attack was imminent but had not counted on bombs from above! Islamic State has become all too aware of being spotted by drones and changed its tactics accordingly. However, this has only had limited success. Jihadi John, being one notorious IS fighter who was finally neutralized by a drone attack as he stepped into his car on November 12, 2015. With not much left of 'Jihadi John' other than an 'oily stain on the ground.'

Jihadi John was behind the killing of American journalist James Foley along with others. His real name was Mohammed Emwazi was originally from Kuwait and moved to England in 1994 when he was six. Mohammed was a member of a secret Osama Bin Laden sleeper cell based in Britain called 'The London Boys', which planned to carry out atrocities in the West. He was involved with a violent street gang who targeted the wealthy residents of Belgravia, Central London with stun guns. He was being tracked by the British Mi5 as a known terrorist. Mohammed saw himself as the victim and on the verge of suicide due to the intrusion by the British security services. Mohammed believed himself to be a victim. He knew Mi5 were closing in on him. So he decided to flee England and join Islamic State. His travelling companion Ibrahim Magag said in an ISIS magazine. *"In the end, we decided to travel hidden in a lorry – controls are much stricter entering the UK than they there leaving."*

The two of them got to France in the back of a lorry, carrying £30,000 with them when they left England. From France they travelled on to Belgium where they shaved off their hair and beards. They also bought new clothes to disguise their identities. They were quite easily able to book flights to Albania, confident that British intelligence would not have shared their details with the Belgian authorities. Despite looking at their passports, the Belgian authorities did not stop them and they were able to board the flights and make their way to Greece. From there, an ISIS fixer helped them get a boat across to Turkey and get across the border into Syria so they could join Islamic State. Emwazi would soon gain notoriety as 'Jihadi John' for orchestrating at least six hostage murders in Syria along with James Foley.

We were told by the head shed to get ourselves back to base. Much to our annoyance, but command could still be jittery at times at to reduce the potential for losses. They would much rather use bombs or even Iraqi security forces. Dead British soldiers was not good politically especially after Afghanistan.

ELEVEN - MADNESS

Barely an hour had passed from our briefing and we were in a helicopter about to cross the border into Syria. It was a warm night so we had the doors open and our feet tucked in as we peered into the inky black night. We were flying over the featureless desert, before banking hard and turning to the east. I caught the outline of several palm trees. Our birds were now hugging the ground as we got in close to avoid radar detection. Trees and vegetation would not only hide us from view but also help screen the noise from the rotors and twin turbine engines. I made a mental note of the terrain as we flew over it, using the map of the area in my head to get a rough idea of our position. Should we get shot down it would help enormously with our subsequent escape and evasion.

This operation had led to a quick battle orders and a kit check. The whole mission was based on local intelligence and an 'eye in the sky.' We only had an approximation of the numbers of IS fighters at the objective which was believed to be fifteen. This included an Islamic State intelligence officer which was our objective. Mi6 had gathered the intelligence and used one a U.S Predator drone to verify it. A drone strike was normally used but the potential for intelligence especially mobile phone intelligence was felt that special forces could both take out the target and gather any useful intelligence.

Prior to our attack an RAF Sentinel had been used to locate the ISIS forces by intercepting communications then RAF Typhoons had been sent in to bomb targets North of Mosul as a diversion. The Sentinel

R1 is now the RAF's sole long range wide area battlefield surveillance aircraft. It is equipped with powerful radar to identify and track numerous targets over great distances, passing the information in near real time. It is based on a long range business jet and entered service in 2008. The Sentinel is based on the Global Express long range business jet manufactured by Bombardier.

We were now a couple of minutes out and time to do a final weapons and kit check. Our birds began to slow down and we prepared to jump off the minute the helicopters wheels touched the ground. The moment we hit the ground we leapt out and quickly made for our objective. It was a small compound in the middle of nowhere. A perfect Islamic State hideout. It had sentries positioned on the roof as well as a roving guard walking round the perimeter.

We made use of some long grass and thick vegetation for cover. As we got close we could hear voices in some of the nearby compounds. I notice that the lights inside were flickering,

We were sure that there would be people looking out or on the roof, but through our NVGs we could not see anyone positioned up there. Undertaking an early morning raid helped, as many fighters would be asleep and reduced potential contact, even though once we were in and shooting, the rest of the fighters would soon be woken up by the commotion.

We had a predator drone keeping a watchful eye and collecting a live video feed of the operation. This would be used by our commanders and intelligence agencies as well as in our debrief later. An eye in the sky meant we had extra eyes that could not only could see the attack from above, but could pass on vital real time intelligence as we commenced our attack. This could be the location of IS fighters or incoming reinforcements. It also meant anyone who tried to make a hasty retreat could be quickly tracked and eliminated if necessary.

I looked at my watch and it was 0215 hours and ready to launch our assault. We would need a quick breach and elimination of any IS fighters we found. The greater the surprise and speed the less chance they would have to offer and form of co-ordinated response.

Walking along huddled down as low as we could get, I caught sight of a IS fighter through the green hues of my NVGs.

The plan was for a simultaneous frontal assault on several of the buildings that made up the compound. The idea was to go in and take out anything we found moving, if we could take the intelligence officer alive, we would. It was highly unlikely he would give us any intelligence unless we could 'persuade' him that working for us was a better option. But, as these Islamic State nutters believed in martyrdom. Which is basically, suffering or dying for your beliefs. This might not sound pleasant, to those in Islamic State it's a great honour. The root of martyrdom is the Greek word martur, which means "witness.

Back at base on giant monitors. The white shapes that represented us could be seen moving up towards the compound. We were no fifty feet from our objective and had luckily still not been spotted.

I glanced over my shoulder to see that everyone was formed up ready to. I used hand signals to direct the operators to the three entry points on the compound.

I was attacking the main target along with Matt and we stacked up at the door waiting to burst in. All three entry points would be breached simultaneously. In total we had eight operators. Two stacked up at each of the entry points and a further two acting as cover.

One by one we got on the radio and said, "In position." Finally, after a minute, I gave the order to begin the assault.

Matt reached out and carefully tried the door handle. No point kicking the door down if the door was unlocked. By chance it was unlocked as Matt gently pushed it open his NVGs probing the room half expecting an IS fighter to open up on us the moment we put a foot inside. I could feel sweat trickling down my face, as even though it was the early hours, it was still very warm. There was nobody in there. There could be someone hiding under the floorboards, but we doubted this and moved onto the next building to support the other two teams.

The remainder of the team had swiftly gone through the building double tapping anything that moved or was asleep in a bed. Thankfully, there was no women or children in this compound. That always complicated matters and tied up operators while they were dealt with and taken out of harm's way.

I spotted the nose of a battered Toyota Hilux poking around the corner of one building. Its red paint had faded in places. It had seen plenty of action judging from the number of dents and scrapes on the front fender and down the sides. This same Toyota had been seen conveying our target around the local area. So we knew we were in the right place, we just had to locate him. Just as I was about to check the Toyota out I heard the sound of an AK-47 opening up just to my right from a roof top. Marc spun round and as the expert marksman that he is fired off a couple of rounds. These hit the IS fighter in the chest and the face. Partially blowing his face off in the process. The IS fighters hail of fire had missed both of us completely. Either he was a lousy shot or could not actually see us in the dark.

The AK-47 ringing out alerted the rest of the IS fighters that they must be under attack and our element of surprise was gone. We needed to ensure our target did not flee and quickly picked up the pace to get the area secured. I ran with Marc into the building we be believed the IS intelligence officer was hiding.

On entering I found another IS fighter inside his weapon spat out a hail of bullets. I opened up firing down the main corridor of the building. Marc did not realise until later a single round had hit his body armour and saved his life. The house had all its lights on, so our NVGs were rendered useless. We quickly continued room by room clearance being all too aware of potential booby traps. There were several rooms off the main corridor and each one would need to be searched and cleared. With our presence now know we flung in stun grenades into a couple of the rooms.

The first flash bang went off with the usual flash and crackle. We moved on to the next room, Matt threw the flash bang in and went in first, he let off several rounds taking out two IS fighters who had only just awoke, probably from the noise of the first flash bang. The IS fighters AK-47s lay on the floor next to their beds. They were promptly killed before they had a chance to grab them and use them on us.

We pushed up the main corridor before rounding the door to the last room, with my weapon levelled as I went in. I saw a man in his early thirties with a long brown beard wearing a black dish-dash. He had more hair on his chin than his head. His eyes were filled with hatred and rage. He had the look of someone who felt we were beneath him and how dare us enter his living quarters.

I had no idea what he would do next and saw he was holding an automatic pistol. Without thinking I did a double tap to the head watching blood splatter onto the creamy brown wall behind him. Before he dropped to the floor. Matt quickly searched him, seizing two mobile phones, while I did a search of the room picking up any papers or personal affects that could be of interest to us. That was the last room and final building out of the three to be cleared. Nine IS fighters lay dead within the compound and another two had been taken out by the Spooky flying above as they tried to escape.

With no time to waste we re-grouped checked for injuries and quickly made our way back to the pick-up point with our helicopter waiting to whisk us away back into Iraq and relative safety of our base. It was an uneventful trip back to base. That is the best sort of journey. With no injuries the target eliminated and a useful amount of intelligence gathered it was a successful op. Now it was time for the usual debrief followed by snap.

TWELVE - SHOCK

Islamic State has been operating independently of other jihadist groups in Syria such as the al-Nusra Front, the official al-Qaeda affiliate in the country, and has had a tense relationship with other rebels. They have had a limited amount of military success with the capture of Raqqa in 2014. Baghdadi the leader of Islamic State sought to merge with al-Nusra, which went on to reject the deal, and the two groups have operated separately since. Zawahiri an al-Qaeda chief has urged ISIS to focus on Iraq and leave Syria to al-Nusra, but Baghdadi and his fighters openly defied Zawahiri. Hostility to Islamic State has grown steadily in Syria as Islamic State regularly attacked fellow rebels and abused civilian supporters of the Syrian opposition. The Russian offensive in Syria has targeted in the main Islamic State. But, Russia has also targeted some of the rebel forces as well in order to aid government forces regaining control of the country since the start of the uprising in spring 2011.

We crossed into of Syria at the tail end of a sandstorm, just as the first rays of dawn light broke through. The ground below was a mixture sand dunes and tall rocky outcrops. We were all on a high state of alert as we entered hostile territory. It was not long before we could hear the sound of gunfire. The shots initially sounded scattered but as we got closer the fire became more and more intense. Tracer fire along with rounds of various calibre began to whip round us.

A round finally found its mark and hit a fire extinguisher setting it off and filling the cockpit with white smoke. Having a round actually finding its mark heightened our situational awareness. Another round whizzed through the open doors just missing all of us. The ground fire seemed to intensify as I saw a couple of RPGs head our way before harmlessly detonating below us. The door gunner was swivelling around firing at targets on the ground below as another round punched through the outer skin and cut through a wiring loom. The cockpit lit up like a Christmas tree as numerous warning lights flashed up on the console. Further tracer rounds whizzed above and below us lighting up the night's sky. The navigator took a small flesh wound as a round nicked his left leg. Things were starting to turn serious. Our bird did not seem to want to fly the same as the pilots wrestled to maintain control. We had no choice but to turn around and head for home. The operation for us was cancelled and handed over to a drone strike instead.

Another round hit the plexiglass on the door and showered us in a shower of hot plastic. The door gunner continued to hammer out rounds at what was believed to be IS fighters below, but it could have been rebel forces who thought we were government forces. Our job was simply to survive and outrun this firestorm that we had found ourselves in.

Another blast from an RPG detonating a bit too close for comfort rocked the bird violently from side to side. Another round pierced the outer skin and hit a hydraulic line, thankfully being deflected instead of doing any damage. The Pave Hawk like the Black Hawk it is based on has three hydraulic pumps and associated systems along with self-sealing valves to reduce leaks. Hydraulic fluid is to a helicopter what blood is to us. A bullet ripped through the bottom of the chopper before exiting out of the open side door. I hung out of the side door of the bird again to check on the other helicopter. It seemed to us that because we were flying in front of the other bird, we were taking most of the fire. Rounds had been fired at the other bird but not one of them had actually hit it. I turned back to hang outside again to try to see if we were finally starting to outrun this firestorm. It did seem that the number of rounds being fired had dramatically reduced.

These Pave Hawks are built to survive; this was the most amount of fire I had ever received in a helicopter even after Afghanistan. Where we had taken the odd round, but nothing like this. The whole ordeal had lasted only a few minutes but it seemed much longer than that. In the air you cannot take cover behind a building you rely on speed or altitude to get away as quickly as possible. As in the air there is nothing for you to hide behind and can only fly through or over a threat. When you can see tracer rounds coming at you, you know that for every one tracer round there is at least another four rounds you cannot see. We continued our flight back to base warning lights still flashing away in the cockpit but our bird was still flying. Finally, we were back at base as we hit the tarmac hard and bounced to a stop.

We quickly got off and as the rotors wound down helped get the co-pilot out and off for medical attention. We inspected our wounded bird. It was as we were walking around Craig noticed I had been hit in the shoulder. As the webbing on my body armour had been partially torn. It was one hell of a lucky shot and a lucky escape for me. You could see several holes all over the Pave Hawk, the odd one was weeping fluid but nothing serious. The plexiglass on one of the side doors had shattered and there was at least three holes in the nose of the chopper. This is where the 160th pilots earn their pay, keeping so cool and collected under enemy fire even while being wounded themselves. Every bit as professional and cool under fire as RAF or Army Air Corp pilots.

Chris looked as white as a sheet. The shock from what had just happened had obviously hit him. I slapped him on his back and he gave a shallow smile. I knew exactly what he was thinking. This was war and you have to take the rough with the smooth. We have a job to do and it can be success and failure in equal measure.

THIRTEEN – SURVEILLANCE

Under cloudy skies, we dismounted our Hilux's and realised we were going have to detour around a rebel position, the last thing we wanted was to get drawn into any form of confrontation with another rebel force. Syria was more politically charged than Iraq in many ways. Iraq we had full governmental support, Syria is a very different prospect. The Assad regime and the civil war is something the government does not want to get directly involved with. Taking sides could lead to further issues with Russia or be seen by the world community as interfering. Our objective in Syria was to only undertake reconnaissance on Islamic State and leave the country, the rebel forces and government to it. Islamic State has used the civil war as a platform to take control over parts of the country.

The Syrian civil war began with the build-up began early spring of 2011 with nationwide protests against President Bashar al-Assad's government, whose forces responded with violent crackdowns. March 15-21, 2011, is considered to be the beginning of the Syrian uprising. On March 18, the protests turned bloody when the Syrian government reacted with deadly violence. Then on 20 March in Daraa after security forces opened fire on the protesting crowd, protesters burned the local Ba'ath Party headquarters, the town's courthouse and a telephone company building. That day 15 demonstrators and 7 policemen were killed in Daraa. As things escalated so did the number of deaths with the death toll at 90 civilians and 7 policemen by March 25, 2011.

The demands of those in the uprising, up until the beginning of April was about democratic reforms, release of political prisoners, "freedom", abolition of emergency law and an end to corruption. This turned towards the overthrowing of the Assad regime.

As protests spread across Syria so did the violence and military intervention. On April 25, 2011, the Syrian Army started a series of large-scale military attacks on towns, using tanks, infantry carriers, and artillery, to try and curb the ever more violent protests, which lead to hundreds of civilians dying. Assad, in his March 2011 speech addressed the protests. He claimed that an international terrorist conspiracy sought to topple his government. During this time, Assad decided to release extremists from the Sednaya prison; extremists with no association to the uprisings. These fighters would go on to lead militant groups such as ISIS and al-Qaeda affiliate Jabhat al Nusra. Creating further problems not only for the rebels but the Assad regime and multiple organisations tried to wrangle control of Syria. Russia would like to see Assad back in power as he is an ally of theirs. The way Russia has conducted itself in Syria has caused friction with the American and coalition air campaign including tensions with Turkey.

We made a diversion of a couple of miles round the rebel force and managed to pass unnoticed. Much to all of our relief. However, this had manged to consume precious mission time. We had a set area to use as an observation post and capture valuable intelligence on an Islamic State training camp. Drones could only gather so much intelligence and over a set period of time. Often Islamic State would take cover from drones trying to hide their operations. Eyes on the ground over several hours or even better several days could yield a much more accurate picture of what was happening at the location. We could also often better identify who was there and what the area was being used for. If needed, we could also guide in bombing runs on live targets before they could move or hide from coalition aircraft.

We reached our OP at dawn on a rocky outcrop overlooking the Islamic State training camp. Intelligence and aerial photographs showed an uninhabited area, but in fact it was surrounded by Syrian Army forces on one side and an opposing Islamic State force on the other. The SAS also had a patrol out not too far from our location looking at another area believed to be a training camp.

Once at our OP we set up who was going to be on sentry while others rested. As Dawn broke the training camp came into view. What looked like a patrol left through the camp gates and headed out on the pack of three pickup trucks. They had a mixture of weapons including an RPD light machine gun which was developed in the

Soviet Union in 1945 by Vasily Degtyaryov for the intermediate 7.62x39mm M43 cartridge. A couple of RPGs, PKs and AK-47s were being carried by the rest of the patrol. It was most likely heading off to try to hold back the Syrian government forces.

We continued to observe the training camp for the next twenty-four hours and watch young recruits going through their basic training. Which seemed very basic, half of them seemed unable to fire off an AK-47 without either flying backwards or dropping the weapon in the process. It did make us all smile then Marc said "You know what Islamic State training sucks." Marc was right. Although through being high on drugs or simply dedicated to their cause lack of talent was made up for by sheer aggression.

With all the intelligence we required captured and passed on. Most likely for air attack we gathered up all out kit to make our way back out of Syria and got mounted up on our Hilux's after a short work the where we had concealed them.

We would use the same route that we had used to come in on and avoid any of the opposing forces. The training camp was not one of the larger camps - more of a small training camp with around one hundred personnel. After a couple of hours of driving we were back in Turkey for the usual debrief before chow, rest and preparation for the next operation we would be sent on.

FOURTEEN – JDAM

Taking shelter in a nearby compound, we could hear ISIS taking on the Iraqi military. A predator drone was circling high above recording the fight. Delta was also engaged in some fierce fighting in support of the small Iraqi force. We had been brought in to laser targets for coalition aircraft. But, instead we needed to go in as a quick reaction force and provide extra manpower. There was about thirty ISIS fighters pinning down the Delta operators and Iraqi soldiers.

The Iraqi's had launched their attack slightly too early after communication confusion and our radios falling over. By going in earlier than expected, we had been unable to get into position they had become pinned down. They were doing their best, but judging by the sound and tone of their voices things were starting to turn bad. We needed to go in and give some fire support. The predator drone feed to HQ was relayed back to us to help us formulate a plan and potential route to take out the ISIS position.

The Iraqi's had already got one fatality and another minor injury, so any plan needed to be formulated and put into practice quick time. The boss quickly came up with a workable plan. The plan was for us to spilt, into two teams; one team of four to flank from the right and then one team from the rear. Using the predator drone to gives us updates on the ISIS positions and help us vector in on them. Delta along with Iraqi soldiers would continue to lay fire down to suppress the ISIS position.

The Reaper is another great piece of kit able to undertake missions of up to 24hours. Manufactured by General Atomics MQ-9 Reaper is known as an Unmanned Aerial Vehicle (UAV) and is used primarily in the USAF and Central Intelligence Agency CIA. The MQ-1 Predator was initially conceived in the early 1990s initially just for reconnaissance and forward observation roles. The Reaper is a larger and much more capable UAV, entering service in 2007. The MQ-1 has been in use since 1995, and has seen combat over Afghanistan, Pakistan, Bosnia, Serbia, Iraq, Yemen, Libya, and Somalia. During February 2002, in Afghanistan armed Predators were used to destroy a sport utility type vehicle belonging to suspected Taliban leader Mullah Mohammed Omar and inadvertently kill Afghan scrap metal collectors near Zhawar Kili because one of them resembled Osama bin Laden.

On March 4, 2002, a CIA-operated Predator fired a Hellfire missile into a reinforced Taliban machine gun bunker that had pinned down an Army Ranger team whose CH-47 Chinook had crashed on the top of Takur Ghar Mountain in Afghanistan. Previous attempts by flights of F-15 and F-16 Fighting Falcon aircraft were unable to destroy the bunker.

With our orders complete and approval from the head shed, we split up into two separate teams and began a climb that was more of a scramble up a loose rock face to get into a decent firing position. The first team came under fire almost straight away and they became pinned down. We were a little luckier and with the help of the feed from the Reaper managed to go round the back of a group of Taliban fighters before opening up. That was four fighters down and what looked like another twenty to go. The other team had gone back down the rock face and tried going in from a different angle with greater success also taking out an ISIS position of two IS fighters in the process.

Delta Force and the Iraqi soldiers were still pinned down and getting low on ammunition. Air support was available, but due to the close proximity and difficult terrain, making use of it ran the high risk of a blue on blue.

The next position the Reaper vectored us onto was a position with heavier weapons, including a LMG (light machine gun) in the form of a PK, 50mm mortar and RPGs. This position was the one that was causing Delta Force the biggest headache. The mortar and RPG fire and been pretty inaccurate. It was the PK that had cut down an Iraqi soldier. The PK is a 7.62 mm general-purpose machine gun that was designed in the Soviet Union and is still in production. It was introduced in the 1960s and used by a whole host of countries around the world.

The IS fighters had a good position with overhead protection, which would have taken quite a bit of effort to neutralise if we had not gone for a more direct attack. I could just about make out one of the bunkers occupants in my sights. The concern was that if we took one out, fire from the PK would start to rain down on us.

Matt, being as mad as ever, volunteered to crawl on his belt buckle and lob in a grenade, if we put down some covering fire. Matt started his crawl on his belt buckle. I put the butt of my sniper rifle into my shoulder lining the scope up and took two short breaths and holding it, before gently pressing the trigger and letting off a shot. The shot went straight through the compound window and slotted an RPG gunner, just before he launched yet another RPG.

The compound was one or two room's at most so quite small, almost a hut.

With fire coming from a new direction the IS fighters PK fire turned on us and we began to fire into the compound. The PK fire was accurate and we needed to come in and out of cover to give covering fire for Barnes. Barnes was now a mere 10 metres from the compound, closing in fast. At about 3 metres, Matt pulled the pin and held the grenade for a few seconds before throwing it through an open window. A hollow blast followed with smoke pouring out of the window and whoever was in that room was now dead.

Matt stayed low made his way into the compound and let off a few rounds to ensure everyone inside was dead. The grenade had made a bit of a mess with blood splatted inside and three IS Fighters lying motionless with one minus his head.

With the small compound silenced Delta Force was finally able to move forward and into the caves, killing seven Taliban fighters in the process. The other SAS team moved into a position so that they could give 'over watch' to Delta Force and the Iraqi soldiers as they finally launched their assault. We held firm at the compound – keeping eyes on for any ISIS movements towards us, although the Reaper that was still flying above us had done a good enough job on its own.

With ISIS cleared from the surrounding area and the objective secure, we were ordered to move out before two F-18's came in and dropped two JDAMs to destroy vehicles kill any hidden IS fighters. These is where teamwork comes in, watching each other's backs, no matter what nation they are from. We are all part of the same coalition with the same end game – destroy ISIS.

FIFTTEEN – U.S. FLASHBACK
Syria 2014

A counterterrorist operation has several distinct phases. The first is getting to the area of operations. At the same time real time intelligence is gathered and analysed by various agencies involved in the operation this continues until the operation is complete. After the raid intelligence is gathered and further analysed. In Iraq it has mainly been the CIA, Mi6 and Iraqi security forces who have gathered the majority of intelligence although other organisations have been involved. Those individuals connected or part of Islamic State and subject to surveillance and capture by other countries such as France and Belgium have added in helping build a bigger picture of Islamic State and how it operates. Preventing several planned attacks in the process.

Once in the area of operations we need to prepare, this could be target surveillance, checking of inner and outer security rings, enemy assets and any likely reinforcements. We had to discuss everything as an assault team and decided best approaches that we are all in agreement with. Tasks are allocated to the various specialists within the team, such as sniper, demolitions, tactical driver and so on. Finally, we undertake the assault, takedown of the objective and once completed a swift withdrawal was essential especially on an operation deep behind enemy lines.

On July 4, 2014, it was just after midnight on Independence Day when a series of air strikes by U.S. aircraft were launched against an Islamic State camp known as "Osama bin Laden Camp." As the bombs dropped twelve Delta operators and Jordanian Special Forces parachuted from Black Hawk Stealth Helicopters similar to the ones used in Operation Neptune Spear. These Black Hawk 'stealth helicopters' had a much lower radar and heat signature. They are also virtually noiseless. Perfect for a more clandestine approach. The only downside is the extra weight from all the modifications. Which means they cannot fly as high as the standard Black Hawk or Pave Hawk helicopters. The Delta Operators all looked down into a derelict and empty compound. It looked as though Islamic State had abandoned it. The main gate to the prison was wide open as were the doors that the operators could see. Some of the windows were broken and the courtyard was overgrown with weeds and brush. The ground was littered with rubble and garbage. They could almost smell the place from the chopper. It smelled like an overflowing trash can.

The Delta and Jordanian Special Forces jumped into the cool night air. The Islamic State prison they were jumping into was believed to be holding several high value prisoners including the captured American reporter James Foley. The prison not a proper prison just a makeshift prison located within an oil refinery about 11 miles south east of Raqqa in Syria. As soon as they landed the U.S. and Jordanian Special Forces blocked off the only main road towards Ar-Raqqah before beginning their assault on the prison. The twelve operators had to fight all the way into the prison against quite stiff resistance. They were assisted by several Jordanian Special Forces lads as well. Sadly, on searching the prison no prisoners were found and it looked they had only just been moved. It would later turn out that the prisoners had been moved about 24 hours earlier.

Delta operators decided to conduct a dangerous but necessary house to house search in Uqayrishah in the vain hope the prisoners may have been hidden there. This was to prove futile. While searching, Islamic State reinforcements from Ar-Raqqah arrived. It was not long before Delta and the Jordanians soon became pinned down by an aggressive force. The firefight raged for nearly three hours with a mixture of small arms and RPG fie.

Rounds were bouncing off the walls and the ground as Delta and the Jordanian Special Forces returned fire. This firefight proved how deadly Islamic State could be when properly co-ordinated and with the necessary manpower.

American aircraft were also fired upon with RPGs but thankfully not one was successful in hitting any of the aircraft trying to aid the Delta Operators on the ground. With no sign of the hostages and an intense firefight that had already injured one Delta operator and one

Jordanian special forces lad. It was decided to make a tactical retreat. By 0300 hours it was all over and several buildings had been severely damaged in the raid. Islamic State had lost eight fighters including trainee IS leaders from Tunisia and Saudi Arabia.

SIXTEEN – DELTA BLOW
Iraq October 2015

On October 21, 2015 a Delta Force raid was launched just east of the Islamic State stronghold of Hawija, in northern Iraq, in the largely Kurdish region of Kirkuk. The mission objective was to rescues 70 hostages being held by Islamic State, due to be executed on the same day as the operation. The prison itself was quite formidable. It was a large compound with bar concrete walls and the floor was strewn with rubble. Delta along with some Peshmerga soldiers would mount an assault to free the prisoners. American led air strikes would bomb the surrounding roads to stop the IS fighters from escaping with any prisoners and leaving them no choice but to fight.

Everyone knew it was a dangerous mission – there are very few which are not. But due to the building and numbers of IS fighters this would be more dangerous than normal. The force consisted of 30 Delta operators and 48 Peshmerga from the Counter Terror Department (CTD). They were flown in by three Chinook Helicopters and three Pave Hawks. The prison was located 4 miles north of Hawija. At 0200 hours the helicopters began to airdrop the force directly onto the target. The initial plan was for the Peshmerga to lead and Delta to act as fire support. However, almost as soon as the forces had been inserted an intense firefight ensued.

The firefight started as soon as forces got close to the prison. The Peshmerga CTD soldiers soon became pinned down with fire from the prison and Delta had to push forward also coming under fire. Once Delta had made it into the prison. They began room by room clearance. Using night vision goggles each and every step had to be fought for. IS fighters barefoot and in long robes, some badly stained ran in and out of rooms spraying bullets indiscriminately as they shouted out the locations of Delta and CTD soldier's. While telling each other to "move quickly." In some of the rooms groups of prisoners were huddled together with fear in their eyes. About twenty of them were ex-members of Iraqi security forces. They had been told it was the last day they would be alive and had earlier had to dig their own graves. These prisoners were pulled out patted down to check they were not IS fighters pretending to be prisoners. Some IS fighters did surrender and were promptly taken prisoner. As well as securing the prisoners the usual process of gathering intelligence was also undertaken.

The bitter firefight continued as Delta made its way through the prison. Taking out IS fighters as they went. After the intense firefight bullet holes could be seem on most of the walls, although some may have been from earlier battles in and around the compound. Garish bright red and cream stripped wallpaper adorned some of the rooms used as living quarters and offices by the IS fighters. Again, mobile phones and laptops were seized in the hope they would yield yet more vital intelligence about Islamic State operations in Iraq. The operation lasted two hours. Master Sergeant Joshua Wheeler had been hit. His face was grey and his eyes were dilating from blood loss and the resulting shock. He was quickly carried to the awaiting helicopters to take him and the rest of the team back to base.

During the raid six IS fighters were killed along with a further 20 wounded.

Four Peshmerga soldiers from the organised local Kurdish Militia were wounded during the fierce firefight that ensued. This raid also sadly, saw the loss of the first American soldier in operations against Islamic State and the first American soldier to die in Iraq in four years. Master Sergeant Joshua Wheeler was shot during the raid and later died from his injuries on October 22 2015, despite the best efforts of medical staff. Bringing home the real danger Special Forces face mounting a war against fanatics. He had followed his training and to ensure that the mission was a success pushed forward into the prison running towards the sound of gunfire. He was hit by small arms fire losing his life.

Joshua L. Wheeler was born on 22 November 1975 in Roland, Oklahoma. He was a was a highly decorated Delta operator having earned 11 Bronze Star Medals including four with Valor Devices. Wheeler joined the U.S. Army in May 1995 as an infantryman and completed his basic training at Fort Benning, Georgia. Wheeler was stationed at Fort Lewis, Washington and assigned to Company C, 1st Battalion, 24th Infantry Regiment until 1997 when he was assigned to Company B, 2nd Battalion, 75th Ranger Regiment.

In total Wheeler was deployed three times in support of combat operations to Afghanistan and Iraq with the 75th Ranger Regiment. Wheeler joined Delta in 2004 deploying to Afghanistan and Iraq 11 times to support various operations. The real sad element is that he leaves behind his wife and four children. Three of his children were from his first marriage. His current wife Ashley Wheeler having only given birth to his fourth son in May 2015.

Wheeler had paid the ultimate price to rescue and protect the innocent. In war people die on all sides. However, for those left behind it is of little comfort. All we can do is ensure that the memories of Wheeler and the sacrifices he made for his beloved country never die. Any loss of special forces personnel if felt throughout the community and no more so than our American cousins which we have fought closely with on many operations and missions over the past ten years. Developing a mutual respect and admiration for each other's capabilities. We still have plenty of banter and call each other names, but we work together extremely well on any joint operation.

SEVENTEEN – ISIS DUSK?

The SAS has been on constantly involved in operations since the end of World War Two. Over the past ten years the tempo has increased and the regiment has needed more staff. The war on ISIS has seen about thirty retired SAS troopers re-join. Not just to take on ISIS but the private market is nowhere near as good as it once was.

The regiment has fought hard in Iraq and Afghanistan over the past eleven years post 9/11. Both Iraq and Afghanistan had their own challenges and in some respects was a learning curve. Special Forces are still supporting Afghan security forces as the Taliban try to creep back into power.

Romanising about war is not something that this book or the first ISIS Dawn has been intended to portray. I have written this book to try and show the bravery, courage and skill of a bunch of highly skilled and highly trained individuals. In war people die on all sides – families loose loved ones be it friend or foe. The hardest part of the job I do is the loss of a fellow SAS soldier. Often these are individuals who are not only young and in their prime, but also individuals with whom you form a different kind of bond. You just do not form bonds like that in normal life. These bonds are formed from what you go through together often relying on one another to stay alive. When they are taken away it is like losing a family member - a fellow brother. It does take a little piece of you away each it happens and without a doubt and changes you. Those that have fought in any war zone have gone through the same mixture of feelings I have gone through. Although, my experiences are not even close to what those in World War I or II went through.

Being in combat does change how you view the world especially after you have watched people die. The small things that stress people out at home such as losing their mobile phone or being late for an important meeting seem so insignificant to me. These things don't really wreck your day; they are merely an inconvenience. Seeing the aftermath of a father being killed in front of his wife and children, a child left without a family after everyone else has been killed.

Innocent civilians being needlessly slaughtered for what reason? Those are the kind of things that wreck your day. Those are the things that have brought me the most sadness and made me wonder why we have to have war in the first place. I now know more than ever, my job is to do anything and everything I can in my small way to stop this happening. Killing people is far easier than I thought it would be. However, those that I have killed have often either conducted or planned to conduct evil acts on innocent people. That for me is enough to justify removing them from this world. They have no intention of changing – they are focused on chaos and destruction. Some of these have become evil through power or money. Using it to inflict brutality on other individuals. I doubt I will go to heaven, but who knows my sins may be forgiven. That is up to God, but for now while I am still on this earth. I can only try to ensure, I keep my family and my beloved country safe and out of harm's way. For that I make no apologies…

As I write this (July 2016) the coalition has trained six Iraqi brigades. These have been called the Mosul Counterattack Brigades or just the Counterattack Brigades. These Counterattack brigades did most of the work at Ramadi and have begun the removal of Islamic State in Mosul where it all began. These coalition trained forces have had input from the SAS, SBS, Delta and SEALs. They are now outperforming brigades that have not received any coalition training. It has helped lift morale and also given the Iraqi government more faith in the U.S. presence in Iraq. Air strikes have stepped up and almost carpet bombing an area before Iraqi forces mount an attack has been found to hit Islamic State even harder. With a greater targeting of deliberate targets such as Islamic State oil, money, bomb-making plants, weapons storage and transportation. This combined with judicious use of special forces has increased the rate at which Islamic State are being suppressed and almost surgically removed from Iraq. To aid in this extra assets have been deployed such as the tube artillery deployed to Makhmur and advanced multiple-rocket launcher systems that have been employed in other parts of Iraq. With this IS Fighters moral especially in Fallujah and Mosul is starting to waver. Their commanders fear they no longer have the same will to either fight or defend that they once had. With a movement of some recruits and experienced fighters to Libya.

For Iraq to stabilize though this means that its political state needs to be addressed so that military success can lead to political achievements and prevent a re-occurrence. It must not be forgotten that Islamic State are the ones holding together various Iraqi groups. This could potentially lead to the same cycle of events post the invasion of Iraq in 2003 leading Iraq to fall back into civil war. In effect this could potentially mean that all this military intervention has been undertaken in vain. With the removal of Islamic State either through them being destroyed or deciding to flee. It could potentially lead to another Iraqi group deciding to take control of parts of Mosul. This could lead to further conflict between various Iraqi groups all vying for control. Effectively solving one problem for another to take its place.

Iraqi security forces would have to take control quickly and ensure it had the political solutions to finally bring stability and an element of peace to those living in and around Mosul.

Another critical political-military problem is the question of the Hashd ash-Shaabi group. Prime Minister Haider al-Abadi understands their importance, especially as they were the ones who halted the Islamic State offensive on Baghdad in 2014. They also have the potential to undermine Iraqi security forces due to being an Iranian-backed alternative military force.

One plan is to integrate Hashd personnel into Iraqi forces something Hashd ash-Shaabi commanders have suggested they will do. The government's idea was to essentially pay the Hashd and control them through the use of payment. If conscription was brought in this may help the matter further. As the Israelis demonstrated in 1948. They found that military service was a powerful method of socialization. The Iraqi military personnel is carefully looking at and considering the Israeli model to think about how Iraq might use conscription to help heal the rifts and build a new, unified Iraqi society. It remains to be seen if this will solve or reduce the issues within Iraq. Although, Iraq is at least still several years away from being able to implement conscription. During that time and the Hashd could continue to destabilize and undermine Iraq and decide that it does not want to be integrated into Iraq. The next six to eight months as 2016 draws to a close may well be the most important part of the war against ISIS. The outcome and future for Iraq very much stands in the balance. I have no idea if stability will be finally found or further bloodshed as the various factions within Iraq continue to fight.

GLOSSARY

AK-47 – The AK47 Kalashnikov assault rifle is more commonly known as the AK-47 or just AK (Avtomat Kalashnikova – 47, which translates to the Kalashnikov automatic rifle, model 1947), and its derivatives. It had been and still is with minor modifications, manufactured in dozens of countries, and has been used in hundreds of countries and conflicts since its introduction. The total number of the AK-type rifles made worldwide during the last 60 years is estimated at 90+ million. The AK47 is known for its simplicity of operation, ruggedness and maintenance, and unsurpassed reliability even in the most inhospitable of conditions.

Apache AH-64 – The Boeing Apache AH-64 is a twin engine four blade attack helicopter with a tailwheel-type landing gear arrangement, and a tandem cockpit for a two-man crew. It features a nose-mounted sensor suite for target acquisition and night vision systems. It is armed with a 30 mm M230 chain gun carried between the main landing gear, under the aircraft's forward fuselage. It has four hardpoints mounted on stub-wing pylons, typically carrying a mixture of AGM-114 Hellfire missiles and Hydra 70 rocket pods. The Apache entered U.S. Army service in April 1986. The first production AH-64D, an upgraded Apache variant, was delivered to the Army in March 1997. Over 2,000 AH-64s have been produced to date with the latest AH-64E. With an AH-64F Apache concept being revealed in 2014.

AV8B – The AV8B was manufactured under licence by McDonnell Douglas and based on the Hawker Sidney Harrier jump jet and later AV8A. Capable of vertical or short takeoff and landing (V/STOL), the aircraft was designed in the late 1970s as an Anglo-American development of the British Hawker Siddeley Harrier. It first flew in 1978 and is powered by a single Rolls-Royce F402-RR-408 (Mk 107) vectored-thrust turbofan. The AV8B is based on the Harrier two, and produced jointly McDonnell Douglas and British Aerospace. The UK Harrier fleet was retired from service in 2010.

B1-B – The Rockwell now Boeing B-1B bomber is a four engine heavy strategic supersonic bomber. It was first envisioned in the 1960s as a supersonic swept wing bomber with Mach 2 speed, and sufficient range and payload to replace the Boeing B-52 Stratofortress. It was developed into the B-1B, primarily a low-level penetrator with long range and Mach 1.25 speed capability at high altitude. It bets the nickname 'Bone' from originally being called the B-One. The initial B-1A version was developed in the early 1970s, but its production was cancelled, and only four prototypes were built. The need for a new platform once again surfaced in the early 1980s, and the aircraft resurfaced as the B-1B version with the focus on low-level penetration bombing. However, by this point, development of stealth technology was promising an aircraft of dramatically improved capability. Production went ahead as the B version would be operational before the new generation of steal bombers. It first flew in December 1974 and entered service in 1986. Powered by four General Electric F101-GE-102 augmented turbofans with 14,600 lbf thrust. With a top speed of Mach 1.25 at high altitude and Mach 0.92 at low altitude. With a range of 5,900 miles and can carry 75,000 pounds of internal ordnance and 50,000 pounds on six external hardpoints.

B-52 – The Boeing B-52 bomber is a long-range, subsonic, jet-powered strategic bomber. The B-52 was designed and built by Boeing, which has continued to provide support and upgrades. It has been operated by the United States Air Force since the 1950s. It has seen action in numerous war zones and has been updated several times during is a long service history. The B-52 completed sixty years of continuous service with its original operator in 2015. After being upgraded between 2013 and 2015, it is expected to serve into the 2040s. Powered by eight Pratt & Whitney TF33-P-3/103 turbofans ach with an output of 17,000 lbf. It has a maximum speed of 650 mph and a range of 4,480 miles. It can carry 70,000 lb of mixed ordnance.

Bell Boeing V-22 Opsrey - TheV-22 Osprey is a multi-mission, tiltrotor military aircraft with both a vertical takeoff and landing (VTOL), and short takeoff and landing (STOL) capability. It was designed to combine the functionality of a conventional helicopter with the long-range, high-speed cruise performance of a turboprop aircraft. The V-22 originated from the United States Department of Defense Joint-service Vertical take-off/landing Experimental (JVX) aircraft program started in 1981. The team of Bell Helicopter and Boeing Helicopters was awarded a development contract in 1983 for the tiltrotor aircraft. The Bell Boeing team jointly produce the aircraft. The V-22 first flew in 1989, and began flight testing and design alterations; the complexity and difficulties of being the first tiltrotor intended for military service in the world led to many years of development. The V-22 entered service with the U.S. Marines in 2007. It is powered by two Rolls-Royce Allison T406/AE 1107C-Liberty turboshafts, each producing 6,150 hp with a top speed of 351mph and a range of 1011 miles.

BLU-82B - The BLU-82B/C-130 weapon system, known under program "Commando Vault" and nicknamed "daisy cutter" in Vietnam and in Afghanistan for its ability to flatten a forest into a helicopter landing zone. It was a 15,000-pound conventional bomb, delivered from either a C-130 or an MC-130 transport aircraft. It was retired in 2008.

BMP-1 - The BMP-1 is a Soviet amphibious tracked infantry fighting vehicle. BMP stands for Boyevaya Mashina Pekhoty 1 meaning "infantry fighting vehicle". The BMP-1 was the first mass-produced infantry fighting vehicle (IFV) of USSR. It was called the M-1967, BMP and BMP-76PB by NATO before its correct designation was known. The Soviet military leadership saw any future wars as being conducted with nuclear, chemical and biological weapons and a new design combining the properties of an armoured personnel carrier (APC) and a light tank like the BMP would allow the infantry to operate from the relative safety of its armoured, radiation-shielded interior in contaminated areas and to fight alongside it in uncontaminated areas. It would increase infantry squad mobility, provide fire support to them, and also be able to fight alongside main battle tanks

E-3 Sentry - The E-3 Sentry, commonly known as AWACS, is an airborne early warning and control (AEW&C) aircraft developed by Boeing as the prime contractor. Derived from the Boeing 707 320B Advanced, which entered commercial airline service in 1962 and stayed in production until the end of 707 production in 1979. AWACS provides all-weather surveillance, command, control and communications, and is used by the United States Air Force (USAF), NATO, Royal Air Force (RAF), French Air Force and Royal Saudi Air Force. The E-3 is distinguished by the distinctive black and white rotating radar dome above the fuselage. Powered by four Pratt and Whitney TF33-PW-100A turbofans, with a range of 4600 miles and a 530 mph top speed. It was produced between 1977 and 1992 with a total of 68 having been made. Long term the Boing 767 will be equipped with the same package as the Boeing 707. The current AWACS is planned to stay in service until 2050 with several upgrades and refurbishments.

DShK – The DShK is a Russian heavy machine gun that came into service in 1938. It is gas operated, with a 12.7x109 mm calibre belt fed and air cooled machine gun. It can be used as an anti-aircraft gun mounted on a pintle. It is also easily mounted to trucks or other vehicles as an infantry heavy support weapon.

Eurofighter Typhoon – The Typhoon is a multirole, twin engine supersonic fighter with a canard-delta wing. It was designed and built by a European tri-consortium of Alenia Aermacchi, Airbus Group and BAE Systems. Political issues in the partner nations significantly protracted the Typhoon's development; the sudden end of the Cold War reduced European demand for fighter aircraft, and there was debate over the cost and work share of the Eurofighter. The Typhoon first flew on March 27, 2004 and entered service on August 4, 2003. It is powered by two Eurojet EJ200 afterburning turbofans. With a top speed of Mach two and the ability to supercruise up to Mack 1.5. It has a combat range of up to 860 miles with three drop tanks.

General Dynamics F-16 'Fighting Falcon' – The F-16 is a single engine supersonic, multirole fighter aircraft, developed for the USAF. It first flew in January 1974 and is powered by a single F110-GE-100 afterburning turbofan engine. It is one of the most manoeuvrable aircraft in the world and is used by the U.S. Air Force Thunderbirds display team and has been exported to quite a few air forces around the world.

JSOC – JSOC (Joint Special Operations Command) is an element of the United States Special Operations Command (USSOCOM) and is charged with the study of special operations requirements and techniques to ensure interoperability and equipment standardization; plan and conduct special operations exercises and training; develop joint special operations tactics; and execute special operations missions worldwide. It was established in 1980 on recommendation of Colonel Charlie Beckwith, in the aftermath of the ill-fated Operation Eagle Claw – See Appendix II

LAW - The M72 LAW (Light Anti-Tank Weapon, also referred to as the Light Anti-Armour Weapon or LAW as well as LAWS Light Anti-Armour Weapons System) is a portable one-shot 66 mm unguided anti-tank weapon. The most common M72A2 LAWs came prepacked with a rocket containing a 66 mm HEAT warhead which is attached to the inside of the launcher by the igniter. It has an effective range of 660ft.

Lockheed C130 Hercules – The Lockheed C130 Hercules is a four engine turboprop transport aircraft with a high wing design. It first flew in August 1954. Since then there have been many variants used by over 70 countries around the world. Originally powered by four 4 Allison T56-A-15 turboprops. It can carry a payload of around 20,000 kg or up to 92 passengers. It is a highly versatile aircraft and has seen use across the world over its 50 years of continuous service.

Lockheed C-141 Starlifter: The Lockheed C-141 Starlifter was a military strategic airlifter in service with the Military Air Transport Service (MATS), its successor organization the Military Airlift Command (MAC), and finally the Air Mobility Command (AMC) of the United States Air Force (USAF). Introduced to replace slower piston-engine cargo planes such as the C-124 Globemaster II, the C-141 was designed to requirements set in 1960 and first the C-141 first flew in 1963. Production deliveries of an eventual 285 planes began in 1965. 284 for the Air Force, and one for the National Aeronautics and Space Administration (NASA) for use as an airborne observatory. The aircraft remained in service for over 40 years until the USAF withdrew the last C-141s from service in 2006, after replacing the C-141 with the C-17 Globemaster III. The C-141 was powered by four Pratt & Whitney TF33-P-7 turbofans, developing 20,250 lbf of thrust each. It had a top speed of 567 mph and a range of 2.935 miles.

McDonnell Douglas (Now Boeing) F15E 'Strike Eagle' – The F15E Strike Eagle is an all-weather multirole fighter, derived from the McDonnell Douglas (now Boeing) F-15 Eagle. It is powered by two Pratt & Whitney F100-229 afterburning turbofans, 29,000 lbf and capable of Mach 2.5 (2.5 the speed of sound). It first flew in

December 1986 and an F15SG version is on order by the ordered by the Republic of Singapore Air Force (RSAF).

Humvee – The HMMWV (High Mobility Multipurpose Wheeled Vehicle), commonly known as the Humvee, is an American four-wheel drive military vehicle produced by AM General. It has largely supplanted the roles formerly served by smaller Jeeps. It has been in service since 1984 and served in all theatres of war. Powered by an 8 Cylinder. Diesel 6.2 L or 6.5 L V8 turbo diesel and with a top speed of over 70 mph, which drops to 55mph when loaded up to its gross weight. It initially lacked any armour, but later version has had some armour protection added against small arms fire.

M4 Carbine - The M4 carbine is a family of firearms that are originally based on earlier carbine versions of the M16 rifle. The M4 is a shorter and lighter variant of the M16A2 assault rifle, allowing its user to better operate in close quarters combat. It has 80% parts commonality with the M16A2. It is a gas-operated, magazine-fed, selective fire, shoulder-fired weapon with a telescoping stock. Like the rest of the M16 family, it fires the standard .223 caliber, or 5.56mm NATO round.

M16 – The M16 is a lightweight, 5.56 mm, air-cooled, gas-operated, magazine-fed assault rifle, with a rotating bolt, actuated by direct impingement gas operation. The rifle is made of steel, 7075 aluminium alloy, composite plastics and polymer materials. It was developed from the AR-15 and came into service in 1963. The M16 is now the most commonly manufactured 5.56x45 mm rifle in the world. Currently the M16 is in service with more than 80 countries worldwide. It has grown a reputation for ruggedness and reliability and was adopted by the SAS over the less reliable SA80. Later the SAS adopted the C8

Panavia Tornado GR4 - The Panavia Tornado is a family of twin-engine, variable-sweep wing combat aircraft, which was jointly developed and manufactured by Italy, the United Kingdom, and West Germany. There are three primary Tornado variants: The Tornado IDS (Interdictor/strike) fighter-bomber, the suppression of enemy air defences Tornado ECR (electronic combat/reconnaissance) and the Tornado ADV (air defence variant) interceptor aircraft. The Tornado ADV variant is no longer in RAF service having been retired in 2011, being replaced by the Typhoon. Powered by two Turbo-Union RB199-34R Mk 103 afterburning turbofans and a top speed of Mach 2.2. It has proved to be a very successful aircraft and still in front line service. The Tornado was developed and built by Panavia Aircraft GmbH, a tri-national consortium consisting of British Aerospace (previously British Aircraft Corporation), MBB of West Germany, and Aeritalia of Italy. It first flew on 14 August 1974 and was introduced into service in 1979–1980.

PK - The Kalashnikov PK is a 7.62 mm general-purpose machine gun designed in the Soviet Union. The PK machine gun was introduced in the 1960s and replaced the SGM and RP-46 machine guns in Soviet service. It remains in use as a front-line infantry and vehicle-mounted weapon with Russia's armed forces, and has been exported extensively. It can fire at 650-750 rounds a minute from belts in 100/200/250 round boxes. Fired from the ground from either a Bi-pod or tripod and an effective range of 1,500m.

Pave Hawk – The Sikorsky HH-60 Pave Hawk is a twin turboshaft engine helicopter and a derivative of the UH-60 Black Hawk. The MH-60G Pave Hawk's is the insertion and recovery of special operations personnel. The HH-60G version is the recovery of personnel under stressful conditions, including search and rescue. Both versions conduct day or night operations into hostile environments. It features an upgraded communications and navigation suite that includes an integrated inertial navigation/global positioning/Doppler navigation systems, satellite communications, secure voice, and Have Quick communications. The term PAVE stands for Precision Avionics Vectoring Equipment. All HH-60Gs have an automatic flight control system, night vision goggles lighting and forward looking infrared system that greatly enhances night low-level operations. Additionally, some Pave Hawks have color weather radar and an engine/rotor blade anti-ice system that gives the HH-60G an all-weather capability. Pave Hawk mission equipment includes a retractable in-flight refuelling probe, internal auxiliary fuel tanks, two crew-served (or pilot-controlled) 7.62 mm miniguns or .50-caliber machine guns and an 8,000-pound capacity cargo hook. To improve air transportability and shipboard operations, all HH-60Gs have folding rotor blades.

RC-135 Rivet Joint – The Boeing RC-135 is based C-135 Stratolifter airframe, and is a four engine wept wing intelligence gathering plane, used by the United States Air Force. More recently three have been purchased by three RAF to replace the Nimrod R1 and MR1. The C-135 is essentially a military version of the Boeing 707 and first flew on 17 August 1957. The RC-135 was ordered in 1962 and was a modified version of the C-135A. A total of nine were originally ordered. In total there is currently 32 in operation, including the first delivery to the RAF. The RAF version is the latest RC-135W Joint River, converted from KC-135R airframes first delivered in 1964. Powered by four CFM International F-108-CF-201 turbofan engines, producing 22,000 lbf (96 kN) each. They are the same engines as used on the current Boeing 737 800.

RPD Light Machine Gun is an automatic weapon using a gas-operated long stroke piston system and a locking system recycled from previous Degtyaryov small arms, consisting of a pair of hinged flaps set in recesses on each side of the receiver. It fires 7.62 mm ammunition from a cylindrical metal container that clips on and holds 100 rounds. It can fire 650-750 rounds per minute is an effective ire support weapon. For firing from the prone position, as well as adding stability when firing, a bipod is fitted to the front of the weapon.

The RPG-7 is a portable, unguided, shoulder-launched, anti-tank rocket-propelled grenade launcher. Originally the RPG-7 and its predecessor, the RPG-2, were designed by the Soviet Union. The ruggedness, simplicity, low cost, and effectiveness of the RPG-7 has made it the most widely used anti-armour weapon in the world. Currently around 40 countries use the weapon, and it is manufactured in a number of variants by nine countries. The RPG has been used in almost all conflicts across all continents since the mid-1960s from the Vietnam War to the early 2010s War in Afghanistan.

The Raytheon Sentinel is an airborne battlefield and ground surveillance aircraft operated by the Royal Air Force. Based on the Bombardier Global Express ultra-long range business jet, it was adapted by Raytheon to meet the RAF's requirements. Originally known as the ASTOR (Airborne STand-Off Radar) programme the aircraft is operated by a RAF squadron manned by both air force and army personnel. The Sentinel is interoperable with other allied systems such as JSTARS and the NATO Alliance Ground Surveillance (AGS).

Sikorsky MH-53 - The Sikorsky MH-53 Pave Low series is a long-range combat search and rescue (CSAR) helicopter for the United States Air Force. The series was upgraded from the HH-53B/C, variants of the Sikorsky CH-53 Sea Stallion. The HH-53 "Super Jolly Green Giant" was initially developed to replace the HH-3 "Jolly Green Giant". The helicopters later transitioned to Special Operations missions. The MH-53J Pave Low III helicopter was the largest, most powerful and technologically advanced transport helicopter in the US Air Force inventory. The terrain-following and terrain-avoidance radar, forward looking infrared sensor, inertial navigation system with Global Positioning System, along with a projected map display enable the crew to follow terrain contours and avoid obstacles, making low-level penetration possible. Powered by two T64-GE-100 turboshaft, 4,330 shp each a top speed of 196 and a range of 680 miles.

Sikorsky UH-60 Black Hawk – The UH-60 Black Hawk has been cemented in history after the books and film 'Black hawk down'. It is a four bladed twin engine medium lift helicopter designed for the United States Army. It first flew in October 1974 and has been used in a variety of roles and variants since then. Powered by two General Electric T700-GE-701C turboshaft, engines it can carry a variety of payloads and be adapted to suit a wide variety of missions. It was designed from the outset to a high survivability on the battlefield. First being used in combat during the invasion of Grenada in 1983.

T-62 is a Soviet main battle tank produced between 1961 and 1975. It became a standard tank in the Soviet arsenal, partly replacing the T-55, although that tank continued to be manufactured in the Soviet Union and elsewhere after T-62 production had ceased. The T-62 was later replaced in front-line service by the T-72. Powered by a V-55 12-cylinder, 4-stroke one-chamber 38.88 litre water-cooled diesel engine, developing 581hp. The T-62 has a top speed of 31 mph on the road and 25 mph cross country.

T-72 is a second generation tank entering service in 1973 and went on to become the most common tank used by the Warsaw pact. Its basic design has been used in the T-90. It weighs 41 tons and has a 125 mm 2A46M smoothbore gun, 7.62 mm PKT coax machine gun and 12.7 mm NSVT antiaircraft machine gun. Powered by a V-12 diesel, with 780 hp and a top speed of 37 mph. Over 25,000 have been produced so far and it currently remains in production.

ZSU-23-2 – The ZU-23-2 "Sergey" is a Soviet towed 23 mm anti-aircraft twin-barrelled autocannon. It was designed to engage low-flying targets at a range of 2.5 km as well as armoured vehicles, at a range of 2 km and for direct defence of troops and strategic locations against air assault usually conducted by helicopters and low-flying airplanes. Normally, once each barrel has fired 100 rounds, it becomes too hot and is therefore replaced with a spare barrel.

APPENDIX I
SAS Originals

What the SAS (Special Air Service) did during World War Two was to revolutionise the way wars could be fought, and in many ways became the blueprint that would be later used by Special Forces across the globe. What was learnt in those early years of the SAS, proved invaluable for setting up techniques and tactics that are still relevant today. The SAS were true pioneers. They made a small yet significant impact during the war. David Stirling's thoughts were to throw out standard military tactics – the SAS was trained to use improvisation rather than follow set military doctrine. This improvisation and adjusting of tactics depending on the objective was at the heart of the SAS successes during the war. They would make do with the kit they had, even borrow or steal kit, even from the enemy in order to accomplish a mission or objective. This is where the true motto of "Who Dares Wins" can trace its roots back to.

Even after David Stirling was captured as a prisoner of war, the SAS continued to grow under new leadership, adapting and growing in size. Until being disbanded after the end of World War II. Only to reconstitute as 21 SAS a Territorial Army unit before becoming a regular unit in the form of 22 SAS based at Hereford. Without David Stirling and the SAS, we would have never have had Bravo Two Zero, Libyan Embassy hostage rescue and countless other incredible SAS operations. All these men are trained to be the best of the best, suffer unimaginable hardship, operating deep behind enemy lines. Using skills and tactics learnt from years of operations.

Whilst the enemy, maybe different, the tactics and types of missions, are not too dissimilar to the ones undertaken by the SAS in World War II. High technology is still no replacement for boots on the ground, who have the ability to react and gather intelligence, in ways that technology still cannot. Highly trained soldiers such as the SAS can help reduce the need for larger scale war and military deployment, by their ability to be used as a surgical tool.

The SAS 'Originals' in the early days had an uphill battle to impress those higher up in command. Even then, at times, military planners did not understand how the SAS could be better utilised, which was a major frustration to the regimental commanders. It was the unconventional warfare that David Stirling had undertaken in 8 Commando that began to lead him to formulate a plan of a more specialised force. At the same time Jock Lewes had similar thoughts to Stirling before joining Stirling in his venture. They both believed that a small group of like-minded, highly trained and dedicated men could cause havoc to the Germans.

Early in his commando training, Stirling was injured in a parachute jump. He spent two months in hospital much to Stirling's frustration. This time spent recovering was not wasted on Stirling and helped to secure the SASs future. He dedicated his time to the actual planning, something he had been unable to do whilst undertaking intense training. He put in place his exact requirements for the regiment from its purpose to the selection and training of the men. Using unorthodox methods that are now associated with the SAS - Stirling took his plan straight to the top. Rather than going through the normal chain of command, where the potential for the SAS was instantly seen. This led to the birth of a regiment that has now become world renowned. It has not been without sacrifice, though, with many SAS soldiers killed in action during World War II and in subsequent conflicts and wars.

APPENDIX II
FAMOUS SAS & SBS OPERATIONS
Operation Nimrod

The sight of the SAS clad in black coveralls and hoods complete with S6 respirator; and equipped with an MP5 sub machine gun - blowing out the windows of the Iranian Embassy, during the Iranian Embassy siege in 1980. Have become iconic pictures that were splashed across newspapers and TV screens in 1980. These pictures of B Squadron, 22 SAS, was in many ways the starting point of the media frenzy surrounding the SAS and other special forces. The SAS at the time were largely unknown and had just been thrust into the public eye.

Operation Nimrod was the siege of the Iranian Embassy in London. At 1100 hours on 30 April 1980, six Iranian gunmen had forced their way into the embassy overpowering a police officer, PC Trevor Lock and taking 26 hostages. The terrorists called themselves the 'Democratic Revolutionary Front for Arabistan' they demanded the release of 91 political prisoners who were imprisoned in Iran. They also demanded a plane to fly themselves and the hostages out of the UK. The police moved in and cordoned off the area and set up sipper teams whilst negotiations were undertaken.

B Squadron was back at Hereford as it was their turn at being the Anti-Terrorist team. They were immediately put on alert and quickly made their way down to London. As they made their way down to London, Mi5 lowered microphones down the chimney to gather further intelligence. On arrival the SAS studied building plans to formulate a potential attack plan if they were given the nod. Negotiations continued in earnest until at exactly 1345 hours on May 5, three shots were heard via the various listening devices and out on the street. The leader of the terrorists, Awn Ali Mohammed codenamed 'Salim', announced a hostage had been killed and if their demands were not met within 30 minutes the rest of the hostages would be killed. Negotiators tried to stall the terrorists whilst a final decision was made on the next course of action. The terrorists had crossed the line by killing a hostage and use of deadly force by the SAS was authorised. At 1907 hours the police signed over control of the operation to the SAS commanding officer and B Squadron completed final weapons and kit prep ready to launch an assault.

Red and Blue team B Squadron, were already in position, ready to go when the order was given to begin Operation Nimrod, at 1923 hours. Four men from Red Team abseiled down from the roof at the rear of the building, whilst another four men lowered a stun grenade through the skylight on the roof of the building. The stun grenade was due to go off as the windows were blown out with explosive to cause confusion. This timing, however, did not match, after one of the SAS team abseiling down became entangled in his rope. As they tried to untangle him, a window was smashed, which alerted the terrorists to the attack. This led to the command, "Go, Go, Go" being given to the SAS teams. With the SAS staff sergeant still tangled up in his rope, the rest of the team were unable to use explosives on the windows as this would have led to serious injury, so had to smash their way in. The three SAS soldiers entered the building after throwing in stun grenades and in the process starting a fire that started on the curtains that proved to be highly flammable and spread to the surrounding room. The ensuing fire, then burst through a window with a very hot flame, this in turn severely burned the entangled SAS sergeant. The team on the roof blew their charges on the skylight, which caused the entire building to shake and sent a plume of smoke high up into the clear blue sky.

Blue Team were slightly behind Red Team as they detonated explosives on a first floor window. Both teams went through the embassy and conducted a sweep using standard room clearing tactics that they had rehearsed hundreds of times back at Hereford. They quickly killed Salim, who was grappling with PC Trevor Lock after he had tackled him, after PC Lock had drawn his pistol, which he had kept hidden since the siege had begun. Moments later two SAS operatives entered the room. They ordered PC Locke to roll clear of Salim and as soon as he was clear Salim was killed by a quick burst of fire from two MP5 sub machine guns. Inside the Telex room on the 2nd floor, the terrorists began firing indiscriminately at their captives, killing one and wounding another. Moments before the SAS burst into the room, the terrorists threw their weapons down and hid themselves amongst their hostages. In what is still thought of as the most controversial incident of the siege - the SAS put the 2 terrorists against the wall and shot them. As they evacuated the hostages, two of the terrorists had secreted themselves amongst the hostages. As the terrorists hid themselves amongst the hostages, one of the terrorists pulled out a Russian grenade. Due to the terrorist being surrounded by hostages a clear shot was not possible. Instead he was pushed down some stairs, where two SAS soldiers quickly shot him dead with a couple of bursts of fire. The whole operation had taken a mere 17 minutes. Five terrorists lay dead along with one dead and two seriously wounded hostages. Fowzi Nejad, the only surviving terrorist, who was later sentenced to life imprisonment for his part in the siege. From that moment forward the thirst for information on the SAS was almost hard to quench, the world and the terrorists knew about the SAS. The terrorists realised that the UK and other countries would use Special Forces to prevent further terrorist acts. The SAS even before the Iranian siege had been involved in the bloody war in Ireland during the 'Troubles' from 1969, undertaking intelligence gathering and trying to track down and disrupt the IRA.

Victor Two

Victor Two

The first Gulf war was caused in essence by the Iraqi invasion of Kuwait. The Gulf War started on 2 August 1990. It was caused by the heavy debts incurred by Iraq and the conflict centred around Iraq's claims that Kuwait was Iraqi territory. After the ceasefire with Iran was signed in August 1988, Iraq was heavily debt-ridden. Most of its debt was owed to Saudi Arabia and Kuwait. Iraq pressured both nations to forgive the debts, but they refused. This leads to Saddam Hussein's decision to invade Kuwait.

The operation to remove Saddam Hussein and his army from Kuwait was called 'Operation Desert Storm' and lasted from 17 January to 28 February 1991.

During the first Gulf War, some hundred thousand Iraqi soldiers died. Many were killed by the intense bombing that took place during the war. The SAS was initially tasked with reconnaissance and lazering targets for allied aircraft to bomb. This was followed by hunting for Scud missiles and destroying them. The Scud missiles were a top priority as it was part of a political game to keep Israel out of the war, which would have inflamed various Arab states and potentially enlarged the war. With the Scud threat greatly diminished, the SAS was tasked with attacking a microwave communication station given the target designation of 'Victor Two.' It went on to become one of the largest Special Forces missions undertaken during the war in Iraq. Over half an SAS squadron of men participated, against around 300 Iraqi soldiers.

The previous day, the SAS had identified an Iraqi military position and sent back a report requesting an airstrike. The position was a mobile Scud launcher that needed to be hit before it moved off. Due to the volume of air traffic and reduced availability, it took some time to get a response. SAS command quickly pushed through a strike with some A10 'Warthogs.' These ungainly looking twin-engine aircraft, complete with their GU8-Avenger Gatling gun, rockets and bombs, made short work of the Scud missile and its launcher. Being behind enemy lines meant the SAS were constantly moving, hunting for new targets.

The next day the patrol split up, with three going off to recce a radar installation and the rest to locate an Iraqi airfield. At around midnight, the three SAS troopers found their target of a radar installation. They were about three quarters of a mile away as they sat and observed the Iraqis. They then began to circle the installation to get a better view. While circling the radar installation, they found a fibre optic cable. These were normally buried feet below ground. At the start of the Gulf War, the SBS had been tasked with collecting a sample of cable for intelligence purposes. That successful mission helped secure the utilisation of the SBS and SAS in the Gulf War.

The wire they had found could not easily be destroyed due to its close proximity to the enemy. The other method, which was the one they used, was to dig a hole and place a tow chain round the cable, before using the Land Rover to pull it out. It was a tried and tested method that had caused complete disarray to Iraq communications. With the cable partially destroyed, it was time to bug out of the area before the SAS troopers got caught by an Iraqi patrol. As soon as first light came, it was time to lay low and go into hiding for the day. That night the patrol moved off, but the ground made it hard going for the Land Rovers, with one of them falling down an embankment and trapping two of the lads. One lad was okay, but the other was severely injured and buried under the contents of the Land Rover. The Land Rover was still serviceable and was dragged out of where it had landed before carrying on. The medics patched up the injured SAS trooper before they continued on their journey.

A few days later, a four-vehicle recce patrol was sent out to locate a microwave communication station, undertaking what is called a CTR (Close Target Reconnaissance). They all knew this target would likely be one the SAS would later attack. That night, four Land Rovers made off towards the target. It was hard going, and after two hours of driving they were making slow but sure progress to the target. It was a dreary, overcast night, making navigation difficult even with night vision goggles. The clouds later started to dissipate, giving a glimpse of the stars and enabling much easier navigation.

After three and a half hours of driving, they had still not yet reached their target. The final part of the journey involved crossing an Iraqi motorway. The arena was a hive of activity, with various Iraqi clearance patrols going on around them, most likely looking for suitable positions from which to launch Scud missiles. The problem with crossing the motorway was that the bridge was unsafe and the motorway had a large drainage ditch running down the side of it, which was too deep for the Land Rovers to cross. They had no choice but to travel a further few miles down a deserted motorway with no lights on, looking for a suitable position to cross. They found a junction and left the motorway. In the distance, the microwave communication centre could clearly be seen, complete with microwave dishes on an antenna surrounded by several buildings. There was a lot of activity at the site and it was a very large installation. The patrol started to head back; as they did so, they noticed that an Iraqi pickup they had spotted earlier had stopped on the motorway and several Iraqi soldiers had jumped out and were walking around the vehicle, which looked like a Toyota Land Cruiser. The SAS patrol stopped and made sure the guns mounted on their Land Rovers could engage the enemy if need be. At this point, it did not look like the Iraqi soldiers had spotted the SAS. The Iraqi soldiers stayed out of their vehicle for approximately five minutes before jumping back in and driving away. The SAS patrol quickly moved away and made it back to base about an hour after daylight.

With the intelligence, and after several messages, a raid on the microwave installation was planned. At 1545 hours, the SAS patrol gathered round a model to receive a briefing and orders. RHQ wanted them to destroy the microwave installation as this was the main control centre guiding the Scud missiles and their launchers. The installation consisted of a building complex with a 200-foot microwave tower. There was a nine-foot internal security fence and 16-foot perimeter wall. Sentries guarded the main gate to the complex. The plan was to drive within a mile of the objective and use the vehicles as fire support. A recce group would then go forward, along with close fire support. The recce team would then guide the rest of the SAS troopers onto the target, which was to totally destroy the building and its equipment. During the initial attack, two anti-tank missiles would be fired – one missile at the main gate and the other at the sentry position. Explosives would then be placed on the inner fence, with the three assault teams affecting entry on the buildings. The building complex had one floor above ground level and two below. Inside, the floors were connected by a central staircase and one assault team was assigned to each floor. Once the Iraqis had been cleared from the building, charges were to be laid. There were believed to be very few military personnel, the majority in the building being civilians, but it was still a dangerous and difficult mission, made more difficult by the SAS already being over 200 miles behind enemy lines.

The patrol commander outlined where the fire support would be positioned and where the assault would start. As soon as that was complete, it was time to prepare for the attack. The final part of the briefing involved the groupings; they were all told, which team they would be on. RHQ had an enormous amount of intelligence on the building, but very little of the enemies' strength.

The afternoon was spent preparing all their kit for the raid, making sure essential equipment was packed and working. At 1830 hours the convoy of vehicles moved out as the darkness and cold set in for the night. After two and a half hours they had reached the main supply route; they held short to make sure there were no Iraqi patrols about before moving into their forward position and splitting up into separate teams. This time, the ditch which had eluded them the night before was filled with several sandbags for the vehicles to drive over. One by one, at a low speed, they crept over the makeshift bridge. Being mobility troop, they had created such bridges in training many times before, but it is always different doing it under battle conditions behind enemy lines. As they got close to the objective, a series of man-made trenches dug in long lines meant the vehicles had to detour slightly before finally coming to their forward position about a mile from their objective.

After doing a recce on the objective, it became clear that there were quite a few vehicles and personnel milling about. It was decided to drive in closer, and it was not long before they hit the main entrance road and began to drive down it, past slit trenches with Iraqi soldiers in them. Further along, the convoy of eight vehicles pulled up against a small escarpment that ran alongside the road. The SAS was now in the middle of a large enemy position, trying to formulate a new plan.

With a new plan of action, the team moved off and parked up behind a large sand bank about 200 yards from the objective.

The tower and its control buildings were surrounded by a wall, behind which would be the second perimeter fence as described in their briefing. It was now easy to determine the damage to the buildings that various bombing missions had done, but not successfully destroyed. A lead scout was sent in to give an early warning to the rest of the team. As the lead scout moved forward, more detail of the objective came into view. As they moved up towards a road, they held short and went into all-round defence. They would need to cross a road and move over open ground to make it to the objective. They then headed back to the rest of the SAS team to report their findings. With this further information on the target it was decided to utilise the vehicles to give flank protection, while the main group, consisting of the demolition teams and fire support, moved up towards the main tower.

They quickly came upon another slit trench covered in a tin sheet, but this was empty so the team pushed forward, before noticing a pile of sandbags in a corner that looked like another enemy position. This position was also empty, so they continued forward another few hundred feet. They were very nearly spotted by a bus, but they dived behind some rocks just in time. Two of the team went back to get the vehicles moved forward before returning to the assault team. Nearby, a fuel truck complete with a browser would serve as a good observation position.

The demolition team started their move towards their assigned objectives as the fire support team got into position. There was an almost eerie silence that made everything seem a bit too calm. The silence was interrupted by a mumbling coming from inside the cab of the truck. The cab contained a young Iraqi soldier of about sixteen years and another Iraqi soldier, both fast asleep. They were soon awoken by the two SAS soldiers, who had no choice but to kill them. Two short bursts of fire riddled the cab with bullets and both the Iraqi soldiers lay dead. The noise of gunfire awoke the Iraqi defences and almost instantaneously, small arms fire opened up followed by Russian SU22 anti-aircraft guns. Red and green tracer rounds were now whizzing across the sky, before ricocheting or impacting the ground. The fire was completely random and it was obvious the Iraqis had no idea where the SAS were. The SAS was now compromised and there was little point remaining stealthy. The demolition teams were busy planting their charges, although the stealth bombers had done a pretty good job and had badly damaged the control centre already.

Small arms fire was coming from all directions as the four charges were placed on the microwave tower. As soon as they were placed, the small grip switches were depressed, giving them a minute and 30 seconds to get a safe distance away. The assault team prepared to leave, but one entrance was blocked by tracer fire. They had no choice but to run the gauntlet, as in less than a minute the microwave tower would come crashing down on them. The team ran like mad to find cover, and luckily no one was hit. Only three of the four charges went off, but this was enough to cause the column to buckle and crash down to the ground, accompanied by a shower of dust and debris. After the detonation, the enemy fire seemed to become more intense, but was only partially effective. The SAS team quickly got into formation and began their retreat from the area. As they drew close to their vehicles, three Iraqi soldiers opened up on them, hitting one of the SAS soldiers through the trouser leg. Confusion led to one vehicle speeding away into the night as the SAS tried to get organised.

The fire support group also needed to withdraw. What was not known at the time was that there were still some SAS soldiers at the actual objective, desperately making their way back. It was going to be a slow fighting retreat as thousands of rounds buzzed all round them. The fire support group and their vehicles joined up with the rest of the SAS soldiers. They now had to punch their way through the various slit trenches and Iraqi soldiers before they could finally get away into the night and relative safety of the desert. Victor Two was a very successful and classic SAS mission. Reconnaissance the next day showed that all the masts had been destroyed and the facility put out of action. No injuries were sustained by the SAS either, which is all the more amazing due to the amount of sustained fire the Iraqis poured onto the SAS.

Operation Marlborough

Within three weeks during May and June 2005, three Delta Force operators had been killed on operations in Iraq. With Delta Force squadrons fielding only 30 to 40 operators, it was not long before injuries and deaths started to have an impact on their capability. The UK Special Forces were asked to assist, but help was initially refused and another squadron of Delta Force operators was flown in. However, Delta Force found itself so committed and the intelligence they had needed to be acted upon so urgently that the British Task Force Black in Bagdad was given the job.

Operation Marlborough was hastily put together and was to be undertaken by M Squadron, who were on their second tour of duty in Baghdad. It was the kind of operation that M Squadron had yearned for. There were some members of G Squadron SAS who helped out, but the bulk of the personnel involved were SBS. It was a hot and humid night as the Special Forces assembled for the operation. There was still quite a bit of tension between the SAS and SBS. M Squadron had been mauled in Iraq back in 2003, losing most of its vehicles and equipment. The SAS felt that the SBS were not up to the job and labelled them 'Tier 2 SF'. At the time the SBS was looking to double in size, adding to the tension with the SAS. The SBS undertook the same joint selection process and many recruits had been syphoned off into the growing SBS. The SBS, though, was thought to have less macho swagger and more thoughtfulness than the SAS. Back in 2004, C Squadron had mounted 22 raids compared to the 85 raids A Squadron mounted in their tour in 2003. This made the SBS look laid-back and less able, even though in reality that was not the case. At that point it was down to the UK-US cooperation, where US SF would often get more and bigger operations and British SF would at times be sidelined.

The team for Operation Marlborough consisted of 16 mainly SBS soldiers, including four SBS sniper teams, each armed with .338 Lapua Magnum chambered L115A AWM sniper rifles. Escape routes were watched by the remaining members of the group in case of immediate emergency or escape if and when needed. The sniper team's mission was to kill Al-Qaeda terrorists wearing suicide vests laden with explosives. They later planned to detonate these vests in densely packed cafes and restaurants frequented by members of the Iraqi security forces. This intelligence had been obtained by Iraqi double agents working for both the British and US Secret Intelligence Services.

On 23 July 2005, the SBS arrived close to their target house, labelled Alpha, with a combination of Humvees and Puma helicopters. US personnel were also closely involved, with a detachment of Rangers acting as a backup force. Some M1 tanks had also been brought in as backup as the operation was in a dangerous neighbourhood. Overhead Task Force Black had Puma helicopters circling, carrying snipers in case the occupants of Alpha tried to launch an attack. A United States predator UAV circled above and had the target building under video surveillance, sending its imagery back to the Task Force Black Headquarters. Listening devices had already been laid inside the building and were being monitored by Arabic-speaking translators. Finally, a command and control aircraft also orbited ahead, linking all the various forces together through a single command. As the SBS moved forward towards their target, a man wearing a suicide vest came running out at them. He detonated his bomb, but it was too early to kill any of the SBS who had quickly taken cover and were crouching down when the vest detonated. The blast caused one of the Pumas that was circling about 100 feet above to rise up in the blast wave before dropping like a stone, trying to find some good air. The pilot, even at the low altitude the helicopter was at, managed to recover by winding up the engines to max power, and he started to pull up within feet of a rooftop. There was no time to dwell as the operation was picking up pace. Another of the airborne platforms had picked up via its image-intensifying camera a man leaving the back of a building and making a run for it. The circling Puma swung round to give the SBS sniper a chance to line up a shot. He lined him up in his sights before squeezing off a round that killed the man instantly. He was subsequently found to be another suicide bomber.

Alpha was now ready to be stormed by the SBS, who burst through the front door and conducted room by room clearance. As they went in, another man wearing a suicide vest ran towards them. One of the SBS opened up on him at close range, dropping him. He had been shot down before he had a chance to activate the bomb and lay slumped up against a blood-splattered wall. The SBS slowly made their way with a little trepidation, fearing that another suicide bomber may make another run for them. This time they may not be quite so lucky. Many of the rooms contained bomb parts and explosives, which meant a grenade could not be thrown in for fear of setting all the explosives off. It was a slow process and no further suicide bombers were found. The SBS withdrew and the bomb disposal experts moved in. The SBS was commended for experiencing what Delta Force operatives had been experiencing as they hunted down Al-Qaeda cells.

The Puma helicopter pilot who had shown expert airmanship and rescued his bird was decorated for his airmanship. The SBS had proven that they were just as good as the SAS and Delta Force when taking on Al-Qaeda.

All stories from **Special Forces** a collection of special forces operations from around the world also by Steve Stone.

Printed in Great Britain
by Amazon